Mary Anne O'Donnell

May 15, 1995

WATCHERS BY THE POOL

WATCHERS BY THE POOL

Nine Lives in Provence

MARGARET REINHOLD

Photographs by William Gooddy

Carroll & Graf Publishers, Inc.
New York

Published by arrangement with Souvenir Press Limited, London.

First published in Great Britain in 1993 by Souvenir Press Limited.

First Carroll & Graf edition 1993

Carroll & Graf Publishers, Inc.
260 Fifth Avenue
New York, NY 10001

Library of Congress Cataloging-in-Publication Data

Reinhold, Margaret.
    Watchers by the pool : nine lives in Provence / Margaret Reinhold
  : photographs by William Gooddy.—1st Carroll & Graf ed.
        p.   cm.
    ISBN 0-7867-0009-2 : $18.95
      1. Reinhold, Margaret—Homes and haunts—France—Provence.
    2. Provence (France)—Description and travel.   3. Human-animal
    relationships.   I. Title
    DC611.P958R45   1993
    944′.9—dc20   93-21935
                                                              CIP

Manufactured in the United States of America

This account of a period of my life draws on many facets of experience.
The houses in England and France, and the cats who have shared
them with me, are based on fact. The characters I have described are
composites of people I have encountered along the way, not necessar-
ily in the context in which they appear. No reference is made or
intended to any living person.

To William and Nora

My sincere thanks to Clare McDonald for her great help with the manuscript

1

There was a time in my life when I lived in Provence.

I had ten cats then, ten beautiful cats and a small dog called Caramel. Apart from the animals, I was alone. I lived in the countryside near a small, thriving market town, full of tourists in the summer. The old farmhouse had been carefully restored by its previous French owners, Monsieur and Madame Belmond, and was surrounded partly by deserted and abandoned fields where once flowers and vegetables were grown for seed, partly by intensively cultivated farms and orchards. In the untouched fields, wild flowers grew and sheets of red poppies in early summer.

The house was solid, built of stone, with thick walls and a tiled roof. It sat squarely on the harsh ground, a wide paved terrace before it, looking to the south. There, in the near distance, was a range of sharp blue hills, pine covered, and in front of them row after row of cypresses stood buffering the land from the cold north wind, the Mistral.

I had a vineyard and olive trees, and a small green garden, shaded in the hot weather by great plane trees. Violets grew there, and English primroses which flowered before the almond trees in the spring. There were irises, lavender, rosemary and thyme.

Being alone, I could keep the hours I liked. On certain days a gardener came, and a pleasant woman who cleaned the house; otherwise, I was free. I could be up all night and sleep all day if I wanted to—but the cats had to be fed and cared for, of course, and the little dog.

The house was calm and peaceful. Although I was on my own I was not afraid in any way.

Monsieur and Madame Belmond had taken great trouble to restore the house in old Provençal style. They had studied books which described how to give old houses authentic period touches, and these were left behind for me to read when they went back to Paris.

The large rooms were uncluttered, almost austere. The floors were covered in old roofing tiles, red, pink and umber. When the Belmonds had lived there they'd had very little furniture. What there was was

To the south of Mas des Chats, in the near distance, was a range of sharp blue hills, pine covered.

dark—antique wooden Provençal chests and cupboards and a huge, ancient table beside the fireplace in the kitchen.

The only unauthentic touch was a pair of mosaics. Madame Belmond, an artist, had designed two large mosaic pictures. One lined the walls of the shower in the main bathroom—slightly erotic, with naked maidens. The other, more successful, lay on the floor of the swimming pool, which they'd had built. There, under the shimmering pale green water, a boy rode a trio of great grey dolphins harnessed together, studded with gold.

I changed the house. I put warm Eastern rugs on the now shining floors. There were tables with surfaces covered in tiles of glowing

8

colours. I filled the arrangements of shelves with brilliant glass and luminous pottery. I scattered the wide terrace with pots of flowering plants. I had the gardener put roses and jasmine and honeysuckle and wistaria against the grey walls.

The place lost its rather severe and chilly authentic character and became cheerful and alive in the present. A few original features remained. The Belmonds had furnished the doors of the upstairs rooms with stable-type fittings—as used for horseboxes. Murderous metal shafts lunged out at unwary passers-by. A turn round a doorway a little too sharp and the projecting arm clutched viciously at clothing and flesh. After a series of wounds, I promised myself to change them to more conventional handles and locks. But this, somehow, I never did. There were other inconveniences, minor and major, to do with electricity and water supplies; but in the main, the house fulfilled the dream—the dream of life in the sun in old Provence.

The cats made the house feel populated. They were attentive and affectionate—although several of them were half wild.

Our arrangement was for mutual care. They let me know that they were looking after me, while I provided the food.

I became very attached to them all.

For a while, those ten cats—and Caramel—were my life-line.

On warm summer nights I used to swim, late, in the pool where sometimes the mosaic dolphins in their gold harness were clearly lit by the moon. Little tree frogs bellowed at one another in an echoing repetitive chorus, fell silent for a while, then shouted again. Crickets shrilled. Bats sailed across the water surface to snap at insects.

In May and June, nightingales sang from tree to tree. The dream house was at its dreamy best.

I cruised slowly up and down in the pool, breaking reflections of moon and stars as I moved through the water.

Out of the shadows, one by one, from this side and that, silently, came my cats, my ten beautiful cats, to watch me as I swam. They gathered round, keenly attentive.

Each considered me thoughtfully. Rosie and Bruno, the leading cats, deeply attached to one another, sat together, exchanging views on the folly of my taking to the water.

Rosie, I know, disapproved greatly of any behaviour which might spoil the perfect appearance of a coat. Fanatically concerned about the state of her own, an endless washer and groomer of hair, paws and whiskers, she was, I think, convinced I was ruining mine.

Bruno was probably puzzled that I'd be so uncatlike as to plunge deliberately into deep water, but in his good-natured and tolerant way he'd accept there was likely to be a reasonable explanation.

Lily was lost in her own world. She stared at the stars and the moonlit ripples on the water and dreamed dreams.

Elegant Hélène, bossy and practical, although fearful, still full of her duties as mother of her beautiful (now fully grown) son Oedipus, shared a corner of my towel with him. After giving me a brief cynical glance which meant '*Quelle folie anglaise!*', she spoke sharply to meek Oedipus and demanded a larger share of the towel. He, who loved but very much respected his mother, quickly obeyed her, moving his long agile body to accommodate her.

Maman accepted the situation quietly. Sensible and strong in her outward behaviour, however nervous she might have felt, she thought it her duty to calm and comfort her child Baby, who sat beside her. But Baby was headstrong and wayward and claimed shrilly that she didn't need comforting. To show her independence, she ran to the pool edge to watch me—then retreated quickly and curled up again against the reassuring warmth of Maman's solid little black and white body.

Monsieur le Gris, stout as a barrel, promenaded up and down beside the pool, now and then giving Bruno a sharp glance, half defiant, half worried. He lived and breathed as Bruno commanded, grumbling all the time. But he was brave. He would stand up to Bruno every now and then. Sometimes he was set upon, tumbled in the dust, squeaking for mercy—even though he was bigger and heavier than Bruno. But he refused to give in.

Nero stared silently. Great black cat, he sat by the pool, gazing intently with his slow golden eyes, willing me to get out of the water and lead him to the kitchen for yet another meal. Neglected and abandoned as he once had been, he had no wish to return to a life of scratching around and hunting for food as he'd had to do in the past.

He was all for having me safely back on dry land.

The tenth cat was Katy. Nervous, small and agile, she was the last to join the group. She was rejected and sometimes chased away by most of the other cats. But she was determined to survive, finding refuge under the car, under tables, up trees, in cupboards. Now she hid under a poolside chair.

Quintessentially French, unable or forbidden to communicate with the others, she led her own life, making little plans, having little adventures, keeping up her courage. But sometimes she went into quiet, deep despair. On these warm summer evenings, while the rest of the cats were busy watching me, she felt slightly more at ease. A cat who sometimes took wild risks, who climbed up dizzying heights and skated on the ice-covered pond in winter, I wouldn't have put it past her to try out the pool, just to see whether or not she was able to swim.

I forgot to mention Caramel. She, too, joined the group, accepted by the cats and accepting them. She sat on a seat and watched me carefully.

The nightingales sang, the frogs shouted, the crystalline water let the moonlight fall to the floor of the pool. The dolphins were lit as if by searchlight.

The cats delighted me and I rejoiced.

2

In the beginning, when I first moved to France, there were only two cats, Rosie and Lily, who had come with me from a house on the Hampshire Downs.

The other eight cats arrived sporadically, refugees from the surrounding countryside. They had been abandoned or thrown out or starved or ill-treated by their previous owners. They found their way to my house in their search for food.

At night, knowing there were many hungry animals around, I put out plates of buns mixed with milk and tinned cat and dog food—a soup kitchen for the needy. Dirty, thin and anxious, various cats arrived to eat. Most of them snatched furtively but fiercely at the food, ate as quickly and as much as possible, and hurried away.

A few of them stayed around. Slowly they tried to establish themselves as members of the family. Of these, eight succeeded in becoming cats of the household.

Apart from Bruno, whom everyone loved, the two English cats disapproved strongly of the French cats.

Rosie, who had a particularly powerful personality, was deeply opposed to taking on newcomers. Right of right in her political views, racist, utterly conservative in every way, she used to express her feelings vocally and in her behaviour.

Both had come from an RSPCA hostel in a Hampshire village.

I went there to find companions for our dearly loved ginger tom, Mews, who died before we made the journey to France. The hostel was run by a Mrs Campbell and the cats, brought in by an RSPCA inspector, were kept in cages in her back garden while she tried to find homes for them. I chose, from the varied collection, Lily and Rosie. Lily sat in a very small cage by herself. Rosie was in a larger cage with other cats and kittens. Even on this very first encounter, their different characters could be clearly seen. Lily, frozen into catatonic despair, sat like a little stone statue, somehow hoping by the very stillness and rigidity of her muscles to keep the world at bay. Rosie, on the other hand, minute as she was, protested loudly.

Lily and Rosie were chosen from an RSPCA hostel in a Hampshire village. Even at the first encounter, their different characters could be clearly seen.

She jumped up and down and stretched her small paws on the wire. Her loud wails implored that someone send for the RSPCA inspector and it was clear she'd continue to wail until she was released from the cage.

Lily persevered in her withdrawnness. She disappeared under a bed on our arrival at Ashford Cottage and remained there for the next three weeks, coming out only at night to eat and use a litter box when all was dark and silent.

And Rosie continued to be a noisy, articulate, demanding, difficult, bossy, superb cat. She had been born into a wealthy home. The owner, an eccentric old lady, allowed her cats to breed, perhaps out of an inability to cope otherwise. When the kittens were born, she simply handed them to the RSPCA.

Rosie had all the confidence and arrogance of some members of the upper middle class, without the slightest self-consciousness. She took it for granted that she belonged to the élite. When she grew up she was a large, strong cat, with eyes like Joan Crawford and a beautiful coat, white, black and tobacco brown. She had large pointed ears and a thick tail, usually held erect. She had a considerable vocabulary and invariably greeted humans and other cats with a trilling call. She turned her nose up at poor Lily for her modesty and her passive fearfulness.

Lily was of legendary beauty, half wild, half mad. She had a soft, pure white coat that was silver in the sun. Her large eyes were almond shaped, the colour of amber. She gave unexpected, uncatlike little cries, little shrieks or squeaks to express pleasure or fear or greeting.

Nancy, the daily help, robust and reliable, looked after the cats and the house during the week when we went to work in London. She arrived every day in a large old Morris motor, bringing her mother, her cat Susie and Sally the dog.

It was Nancy who gave the cats their taste for fish and so ruined their eating habits for life. They considered, ever afterwards, that a day without fish was a day wasted, a day ruined, a non-day, a day of profound deprivation—and the fish must be coley. Nancy, when she arrived with her Mum, brought a bowl of cooked coley which Rosie and Lily devoured. Nancy's Mum was very old and very slight. She talked gently to Lily and Lily listened. Lily was even prepared to go towards Nancy's Mum and sidle up against her thin and fragile legs.

But of all the creatures who surrounded Lily, she loved Mews best. It was a mutual love. She cuddled against him. They slept on the same blanket. They played wild games together in the thick clumps of

Mews, our dearly loved ginger tom, knew from his daily walks where the badgers had been, and the deer and all the small animals of the countryside.

daffodils under the apple trees. Every day she waited for him to return from his outings, long walks during which he inspected the neighbourhood, gathering in the news in detail of all the night's happenings. Mews knew, I'm sure, where the badgers had been and the deer and all the small animals of the countryside. After his inspections, he returned home unhurriedly, marching up the slope of the drive with

15

majestic tread. Lily saw him from afar, silhouetted against sky and trees, and went quickly to greet him. She was desolate when he died. She searched endlessly for him, going again and again to all the places where he liked to lie—a patch of dried grass behind the greenhouse, a bench in the tool shed, a little hollow under the pine trees, his basket in the glassed-in porch beside the kitchen. I went with her on some of her searchings. I saw her anxious eyes as she looked here, there and everywhere, never, of course, to find him again. One day she and I were walking up the drive together when Rosie happened to come out of the house. For a moment, her distant silhouette resembled Mews —a cruel illusion. Lily stopped and stared. Then she bounded forwards —only to fall back in crushing disappointment as she recognised Rosie. After this, she gave up her search and took to lying in Mews' basket day after day, silent and withdrawn. When the move to France was planned I promised each cat they'd find a French beau. In Rosie's case this promise was fulfilled, but Lily remained forever a loner.

3

Some weeks before Lily and Rosie and I were due to leave for France a distant neighbour and his wife came strolling up the drive at Ashford —a casual call while walking their good-natured dog, Kate. We stood for a moment in the late summer sunshine.

'So you're really leaving us?' asked Bernard in his kindly way. 'You really mean to leave all this?' As he gestured towards the charming house, the deep fields of corn in which it stood, the great beech hedge which surrounded it, the wide stretch of grass, the roses and apple trees and the wooded hangers behind, my heart sank. I followed his finger as he pointed and felt a sharp sadness.

'Yes, I'm going to France,' I said. Then his eye caught Rosie and Lily who were just coming out of the house at the other end of the drive to take the air.

'And what about the cats?' he asked.

'They're coming too.'

'Taking them with you?'

He sounded surprised and disapproving. His wife, always severe, echoed his words and tone. My apprehension increased.

That night I had a dream. There were times when, in my sleep, I dreamed about the cats. They represented, I suppose, some aspect of myself, my life, my childhood—small helpless beings at the mercy of great forces.

Such dreams came, as a rule, when I was anxious.

In my dream, that night, I was breaking the news to Rosie and Lily. In the dream, the cats used human speech and were as articulate and informed as humans, each in her style. This caused me no surprise.

We were all walking together across the lawn at Ashford.

'Rosie and Lily,' I said apprehensively, 'we're leaving here. I've sold this house. We're going to live in France.'

I knew they wouldn't be pleased but Rosie's reaction was, as usual, exaggerated and dramatic.

'France!' she cried. 'The other side of the Channel! Don't you realise we'll never be able to come back?'

We were all walking together across the lawn at Ashford.

'I don't see any reason that we might want to come back,' I said nervously. 'It's a lovely house in a lovely place.'

'But *this* is a lovely house,' cried Rosie, 'we're happy and settled. We love this house and the field which you like to call a garden and the cornfields around us and the woods.

'France!' she went on at the top of her voice. 'Don't you know that civilisation ends at Dover? Haven't you heard they eat frogs—and *are*

Lily was soon absorbed in her pleasurable little pursuits among the fallen leaves.

frogs—and garlic and snails? What are *we* going to eat? Have you thought of that? What about our coley? What about our High-Fi and Whiskas?'

'Rosie, calm down,' I said. 'There'll be everything we need. There'll be olive trees and lavender. There'll be dry hills and hot sunshine and no rain for months and months . . .'

'So you're taking us to a desert? You want us to die of heat stroke and thirst? Thank you *very* much. Did you hear that, Lily? She's taking us to a desert. You know how you hate the heat!'

Lily sighed. 'Oh dear, oh dear, oh dear . . .'

'Rosie,' I said firmly, 'there'll be water. In fact there's a stream which runs all round the garden and a swimming pool . . .'

'So we're going to drown, then, are we? One false step and we'll be in the river or the pool. I hope you realise neither of us can swim. I disapprove of the whole idea and I hope you'll have the sense to cancel.'

I heard Lily sighing again as she drifted across the grass. But soon she was absorbed in her pleasurable little pursuits among the fallen leaves.

'Be sensible, Rosie. We'll all enjoy France. You and Lily might find some company. There's no one here for you. It's too isolated.'

'I won't hear a word against Ashford,' cried Rosie. 'You'll never find a house better than this one—and what about my doctor? I trust Mr Richards. What are we going to do for a doctor?'

Rosie was voicing my fears. How would the cats adapt to a completely different climate? Would there be a good vet nearby? Would there be a vet at all?

Courage.

'Why are we going?' asked Rosie.

'I must change my life. I need to make a new start. I see a better life in France.'

'What do you see?' she asked.

'I see sunlight. I see open doors. I see you and Lily sitting in the sun in an open doorway.'

'And how shall we get there?' demanded Rosie.

'By air,' I said, 'we'll travel in an aeroplane. You'll enjoy the flight,' I told her. But poor Rosie didn't hear because she'd fainted.

At this I woke. Daylight reassured me. The cats would settle down in France, I'd make sure of that. They would be all right—but would I?

4

Before I knew that Air France allowed small animals in baskets or boxes to accompany their owners in the cabin of the aircraft I had anxiously considered other possibilities—cars, trains, even the hiring of a small van.

Then, at the airport in Toulouse, while waiting for our flight back to London, William and I sat next to a woman who had two small children and a little grey poodle. The poodle and the children ran about the airport lounge tethered to one another. They tripped up unwary passengers whose eyes were fixed on distant information panels. No one noticed or cared.

There came the muffled announcement of the imminent departure of a flight to Paris. The woman next to me sprang to her feet and summoned children and dog.

'Is the poodle going with you?' I asked.

'Of course.'

'How is he travelling?'

'With us, of course.'

'You can take him with you in the cabin?'

'Yes.' Air France allowed that, provided the animal accompanying a passenger was small enough to be carried in a basket or box.

The poodle was stuffed into a basket, the children were stuffed into their coats. Magazines, chocolate, toys disappeared into a bag.

They were off.

A solution had been found for Rosie's and Lily's journey.

Very apprehensively I made preparations. First, vaccinations and health certificates. The cats grumbled furiously. So many visits to the vet—quite unnecessary, thought Rosie.

She howled louder than ever on her way to and from Mr Richards' surgery. Lily simply removed herself from the situation, pretending it wasn't happening, thinking about other things—her appointment with the badgers that evening, her visit to fox country in the north.

She hummed lightly to herself and tried to escape.

But there was no escape. We were all quite definitely going to France.

The night before the journey they had to be confined to the house. That was difficult in itself since they were used to going in and out through the cat door. They made every effort to get out and complained bitterly.

That night, a bright moon shone. Lily, Rosie and I, imprisoned in the house, peered out from the upstairs windows. We saw, on the moonlit grass, for the last time, the two badgers we knew so well, snuffling round the little tree where the nut baskets hung for the birds. They were eating the fallen nuts and the biscuits and bread I'd put out for them. They grunted with pleasure. The bright moonlight fell on the white and the black of their heavy bodies. The two cats and I stared down at them. Then a fox ran fast across the lawn, black shape, blue moon shadow, and vanished into the fields.

Goodbye to the badgers, to the foxes, to the loved house under the wooded hills.

5

Early in the morning Mr Clarke drove his taxi to the door. We bundled the reluctant cats into strong cardboard RSPCA cat carriers, obligatory on the flight. Strong as these boxes were, they were not solid enough to hold Rosie and Lily. They fought like wild tigers, tearing at the sides and roofs of the boxes which seemed, under their powerful claws, to be made of flimsy paper. The first stop was at the vet, where Mr Richards gave them supposedly tranquillising injections. These had no effect. If anything, they became even more frenzied. At the airport, where William was waiting for us, the boxes had to be replaced by new ones.

Inside the airport, a further hazard. The young security officer in charge of screening hand luggage quite rightly said he was afraid he must glance in the boxes to ensure we were carrying cats and not explosives or guns.

A Cassandra of a woman security officer accompanied him.

There was some discussion as to how best to undo the boxes.

Lily and Rosie, making the most of the situation, tore even more wildly at their prisons and howled at the tops of their voices.

Cassandra said, heavily, 'If they get out, you'll never see them again.' She gestured largely towards the vast open spaces of the halls and runways of London Airport.

'I'm afraid I must look,' said the young man unhappily.

'On your head be it,' said Cassandra ominously.

Very cautiously we opened a tiny chink in the roof of each box.

The young man could certainly see heaving cat but there was no hope of seeing whether the boxes contained anything else. He felt, however, he'd done his duty. 'Right,' he said with some relief. Then we bound the boxes with heavy brown sticky tape, going over and over and round and round. Finally, they were secure. We could carry two bumping boxes on board the aeroplane.

As the aircraft took off, Rosie screamed. Lily, on the other hand, seemed, alarmingly, to have collapsed. She was still and silent throughout the journey. But Rosie went on hammering and thumping away with only brief pauses to gather her strength.

At last, we arrived.

Marseille airport has an advantage over other airports in that, after passing the immigration officials, passengers walk out into freedom. There are no customs officials to examine hand luggage. No matter what is carried into the country in hand luggage, no one interferes. Drugs, firearms, cats, no one asked what was in the cardboard boxes. No one demanded the health certificates, the entry permits of the cats.

We took them straight to the hired car and felt intense relief. Once safely in the car, we opened the boxes and drove away.

Slowly, in the late October sunlight, taking the National 7 rather than the motorway, we made our way towards our new home. We went north among vineyards and olive groves through quiet villages and over the Alpilles. On this journey Rosie and Lily slept at last.

———————◇———————

The house was empty. There was, as yet, no furniture, except for one large bed. William stayed one day and went back to England. Lily, Rosie and I moved from dusty room to dusty room across what seemed acres of the old red tiles. We stared out at the little garden, at the cypresses and the blue Alpilles beyond. To the right and left of the house were the *collines*, shallow hills covered with rough, tough, heathy vegetation and little pines.

The cats were imprisoned for at least ten days so as to become familiar with their new home. In the empty house they were restless and depressed.

The old house, brooding over its own two centuries of existence, shut us out of its past. The thick walls had sheltered generations of strangers whose births, lives, deaths were to be forever secret. But the day came at last for the cats to be let into the garden. I watched them as they investigated every blade of grass, every stone, every bush. I felt lonely and anxious. It was not easy, I discovered, to be an exile.

'It's your decision,' William had said, 'it's what you want.'

In the early morning, Rosie, Lily and I went for a walk in the vineyard. The cats followed me in single file as they used to do when we walked in the fields around Ashford Cottage. The air was clean

24

and cold, the light brilliant, falling like a knife on the blue Alpilles. We pottered among the vines thinking our private thoughts. The cats sniffed the air with their sensitive nostrils—alien smells, alien plants, alien earth.

'Why are we here?' they seemed to ask.

Why indeed? I asked myself the same question.

At last the furniture arrived. Two Englishmen, Harry and Jeff, appeared early one morning without warning. They refused to take their large van round the sharp corner where cypresses narrowed the little road. I had to ask the builder's assistance. He lent us a small truck and a few of his men. Furniture, books, pictures, carpets, glass, lamps, a huge aspidistra and a maidenhair fern, mirrors, dustpans and china were ferried from van to house all day long. Harry and Jeff worked like beavers. Rosie and Lily took off and spent the day on the hillside, watching, concealed. Harry's and Jeff's calm voices, their unhurried and cautious manners, their Englishness, brought nostalgia. They communicated with the builder's excitable men in the way Anglo-French communications must have taken place for ten centuries. The hysteria level dropped to zero.

By evening the furniture was in position. A dozen or so huge cases of boxes and ornaments, china and glass, pictures and papers and old photographs and junk stood in the *atelier*, Madame Belmond's barn-like studio. Harry and Jeff took showers, ate eggs and bacon, cake and tea—all I could provide—slept on mattresses in the guest room and left, calmly, in the morning.

Rosie and Lily returned from their hide-out on the hillside to eat their evening meal. Both were delighted to see the furniture.

Rosie, without further ado, settled contentedly into her familiar chair.

————————◇————————

The first night I was alone at the house I saw a small elderly man in a navy-blue beret come into the garden, led along by a cheerful dog at the end of a short chain. This turned out to be my nearest neighbour, Monsieur Corbet, a local farmer, with his dog Dick. His land lay to the east of my house, separated from mine by a small canal.

Monsieur Corbet clutched in his free hand a small bit of paper, not much larger than a postage stamp, which, after we'd greeted one another, he handed to me. On it he'd written his telephone number in thin spidery ink.

He beamed at me. 'If you need anything, we're there . . . my wife and I . . .'

He gestured across his field of French beans towards his *mas*. 'Don't hesitate . . .' He repeated this message several times in a loud voice.

It was some time later that I discovered he was very deaf. He and his wife turned out to be wonderful neighbours, warm and generous.

'They are darrleengs,' my house painter, who knew them well, told me.

And they were darlings.

I became close to them in time and was fond also of Dick the light-hearted dog and Frisquette, their bad-tempered cat.

6

The winter, which seemed long, slowly ended. Workmen, busy for weeks, went away at last. Rosie and Lily returned from the hillside where they had hidden themselves during daylight hours, while walls were painted white, a roof was retiled and Madame Belmond's *atelier* turned into a pleasant sitting-room.

The house took on its warm and easy character. Spring came. The almond trees flew into blossom. Small blue musk-hyacinths appeared among the dried grasses of the fields. Now the doors and windows were opened to the sun. Rosie and Lily sat in an open doorway, the sun warming their coats.

Then, suddenly, one day, the Mistral blew again with great rushes of freezing air, bringing the smell of ice and snow from the high mountains. The cats stayed indoors all day, heads down. Towards the late afternoon, the wind dropped. We walked in the vineyard. A brilliant light lay on the hills. I looked to the south, shivering in the cold air, longing for the summer.

Two strange cats came unexpectedly through the laurel hedge to join us—two very young cats with coats soft and fluffy as kittens. Both, it was clear, were part Siamese. One was pure white with bright blue Mongolian eyes. The other, blue eyed also, was rounder, more solid than the timid white. His coat shaded from cream to white and cinnamon brown. His ears were dark brown, his profile noble, sloping forehead meeting nose in a pure straight line. Two patches of white lay on either side of his nose and in the centre of his forehead was a small circle of white hair. His brown paws were tipped with white as if he were wearing white gloves and shoes. He had a slight squint—and the combination of azure, squinting, oval eyes, white, brown and beige fur and his round babyish body made him look touchingly comic. Both little cats ran forward, trustingly, to greet us.

Rosie was furious and frightened. She insisted the cats should be sent packing. They would only go when I shouted and threw a handful of gravel at them.

At supper time they turned up again. They rushed into the kitchen

Bruno, a little brown cat who would delight us with his clowning, his affectionate heart and his intelligence.

where Rosie and Lily had just begun to eat. Elbowing the older cats away, the newcomers began to gobble the food as if they were frantically hungry. Rosie gave a loud shriek, begging me to get the cats out of the house.

Easier said than done. The little cats licked the plates clean in a moment and shouted for more.

Rosie screamed again, making Lily run under a chair.

All was chaos and dismay.

We didn't know, then, that we had with us in the kitchen a cat that was to grow up to be the leader of a group still to be formed—a cat that would delight us with his clowning, his affectionate heart and his intelligence. We had there a supreme comedian, a brave soldier, Robin Hood, Romeo, a top cat, a manager, a proprietor, prime minister, King cat. We had a cat, the little brown cat, who was to be the light of our lives—at least Rosie's and mine . . .

Not understanding the rare and precious nature of the little cats, Rosie and Lily and I resisted accepting them. But they'd decided to stay with us. They were determined to stay.

If I pushed them out of a door, they'd scramble in at a window. If they were put out of a window, they'd be in at a door. Stones and harsh words hurled at them produced only a brief withdrawal. At night, they found their way into a bedroom which opened on to the terrace where the door was left ajar. There they slept in each other's arms—a sad pair of waifs.

Rosie and Lily gradually became accustomed to them—and they became less frenzied. I discovered they were refugees from a neighbour's house where there lived a large Arab-Spanish family. Madame Malika, born in a village in the deep Sahara, had left her first husband. She had taken her four children and come to live in France with José, a Spaniard from Valencia. He, too, had children by his former wife.

Now she was about to have another child. It seemed her doctor had told her—or perhaps her friends—not to have a cat about the place during her pregnancy. Cats may, rarely, suffer from a disease which can be transmitted to a human mother and child. She was afraid, also, that when the baby was born the cats might sit on its face and suffocate it.

The little cats had been acquired to amuse her other children. Now they were chased away.

In the end I was feeding them regularly and caring for them. Their joining the household was a *fait accompli*.

I went round to Madame Malika and proposed a deal. This was accepted. I paid a sum of money and the cats were officially mine.

'What do you think?' I asked Rosie and Lily.

Rosie intimated that in principle she was against new immigrants but she was prepared to make an exception in this case.

Lily simply sang one of her fey songs and thought of other things.

I named the little cats Bruno and Blanco and the house, Mas des Chats.

7

A young white horse lived in a field behind my house—a mythical, lonely animal of legends and heroes. He was called Jasmin. He came from the Camargue and had been won in a raffle at a country fair by the farmer's youngest son.

Jasmin lived alone. He was without shelter in all weathers—exposed to violent storms, raging Mistral, the relentless Provençal rain. He stood stoically with his back to the wind, enduring. But he did have a few trees to shade him from the summer sun.

His field was too small for there to be enough grass to feed him and too small for a good gallop. What grass did grow, after rain, he tore up immediately and ate voraciously, leaving space for weeds to take over.

The farmer threw cabbage leaves and tired lettuces over the fence. Jasmin munched them.

He had almost no contact with any other living creature.

Passing people, the farmer, his wife and sons may have spoken to him as they went by. But in all the years he lived beside us in the field I never saw anyone stroke him or take any care of him except once, when he'd injured his knee. Even then, I had to point out to the farmer that Jasmin was limping and in pain.

He was unschooled and unshod, a wild horse of the Camargue.

To the farmer, he was a piece of property, like a plough or a mowing machine.

I decided that Jasmin's life was bleak and empty and that he needed cheering up.

Twice a day I gave him a basket or bowl of dry bread mixed with carrots and apples. Sometimes I gave him a sheaf of freshly cut grass which he loved. I took the grass from beside the stream where it grew green and thick.

After a while, when Jasmin saw me in the garden he would come running to the corner of the fence and call—a shrill peremptory whinny. He could tell the time precisely. At 9 a.m. and 5 p.m. he stood at the fence, waiting for his refreshments. He ate carefully, wasting nothing, like many hungry animals. He searched out the last shred of carrot and apple, the last crumb of bread, meticulously turning over the fallen leaves in case some morsel had escaped him.

When I took the food to Jasmin, the cats came with me. We all stood around, watching him eat.

I felt sad for Jasmin, whose life seemed wasted—or at least impoverished. So little was made of it, at that time.

8

Nero—or Neron as the French preferred to call him—attached himself to the household a little while after the Siamese brothers became residents.

The name Neron, as written on his health certificate by the vet, implied he was called after the Roman emperor. He *was* kingly and noble, but I named him Nero because he was all black, just as the brown cat was named Bruno and the white Blanco.

He arrived as an occasional visitor in search of food. He was a scraggy, filthy, rangy cat, his coat dull and worms clearly visible in the fur under his tail.

As he became accustomed to receiving a meal, his visits were more regular. Then he understood he could have food whenever he needed it. He was never humble, never begging but, in the beginning, nervous and insecure.

When he realised he was welcome and kindly received he became arrogant and possessive. He was clearly badly educated, accustomed to hunger and unused to complicated human living, I thought. I imagined him talking with a thick Provençal accent (if talking at all since he seemed strangely inarticulate, although intelligent, like one of those children brought up in the jungle by apes or wolves).

But I discovered soon that he *was* used to men, only men who behaved strangely towards him. There were two men who lived together as tenants of Monsieur Mabeille, the neighbouring farmer, in part of the old, rambling, converted farm buildings to the north of my house. They must have been fond of Nero, as he returned to them from time to time, but they also abused and neglected him. When they later moved from the farm, they abandoned him. It was Giselle Mabeille who told me about them.

Mademoiselle Mabeille, Giselle, was a member of the huge family of Mabeille who lived in various houses on the farm and in the neighbourhood. Her father had been a wealthy man owning many properties —houses and land. When he died, the houses and fields were divided among his several children. His wife was an invalid and almost all the children were disturbed in some way, if not actually ill themselves. Giselle *was* ill. I was told by many people that she'd been a beautiful and intelligent child, spoilt by her father. She became eccentric as she grew up and the eccentricity intensified gradually as the years went by. She quarrelled with her brothers and sisters. They washed their hands of her. She lived with her dotty old aunt in a ramshackle house among the farm buildings. She was lonely. She was often despairing. Sometimes she paid a visit to my house.

The first visit took place in early summer, late at night, my first summer in Provence.

I was in the kitchen, washing dishes at the sink. Suddenly I noticed the cats showing signs of alarm. I heard nothing. Lily retreated under a chair. Rosie sprang to a windowsill and stared out.

She let me know we had a visitor, but that it was no one we knew.

I went to the door and looked to see who it was. There she was, giggling, nervous. She said nothing. I suddenly realised who she must be, having heard about her from my neighbours the Corbets.

'*Bon soir,*' I said.

'*Bon soir, Madame.*'

A radiant smile on a strangely young face, an outstretched clumsy arm, a clutch of weak, damp fingers. She said nothing about who she was, what she wanted.

The Corbets had said, 'Never let her in. You'll never be rid of her if you do.'

I said, 'You are Mademoiselle Mabeille?'

She beamed, radiant again. The moon had risen. In moonlight and lamplight I saw her plump, smooth, tragic face, laughing—mouth open to show small, even teeth. Her eyes were blue and shining—hiding her dark inner world. She fell silent. I also hesitated. At that moment Nero appeared, and lo and behold he rubbed his body against her legs where wrinkled stockings straggled down.

'Oh,' she cried excitedly, 'Vladimir is here!'

She bent awkwardly to stroke him. He accepted docilely her vague affection.

'Vladimir?'

'Yes! Vladimir! Or . . .'

Doubt clouded her face.

'Is his name Vladimir . . . ? I'm not sure . . .'

Her thoughts stumbled.

'Some musician,' she said.

I tried to be helpful.

'Yes! There are musicians called Vladimir. Vladimir Askenasi—Vladimir Horowitz . . .'

She was doubtful still.

I said, 'It's late. Perhaps you should be at home. I'll take you. I'll come with you.'

She'd come across the hill—a rough path full of brambles and old leaves among the scrub oaks and pines.

There were wild white flowers. They seemed to float in the moonlight.

We went together carefully.

'You know him, Vladimir?'

'Yes! Yes.' And she told about the two men, her neighbours, to whom he belonged.

Jasmin, the white horse, knew her too, it seemed. He ran to the edge of his field, leaned over the fence and called with his excitable neigh.

White flowers, white horse in the moonlight, white rushing water in the stream and the gentle madness of this woman made unreal the night stroll.

'Not Vladimir!' she said, suddenly. 'Vivaldi!'

Vladimir, Nero, Vivaldi had accompanied us. He, too, seemed familiar with Jasmin, with the irregular stony path.

'Vivaldi?'

'Yes—that's his name, Vivaldi.' She was sure now. I was intrigued by the two men who gave him his name.

'Where is your house?'

She gestured vaguely. We were almost at the farm buildings.

'Come and see me again,' I said. 'In the daytime.'

She smiled radiantly once more and slightly bowed.

'*Merci, Madame!*'

'Good night.'

For some time Nero dominated the scene at Mas des Chats with his violent aggression, his passionate jealousy, his possessiveness.

'Good night!'

We waved to one another.

Vivaldi or Nero returned with me. He ran ahead in little spurts of speed. He stopped to sharpen his claws. He seemed very pleased, very cheerful.

A month or two later he had become a problem. By now his owners had abandoned him. They had gone away, leaving him behind. He lived at Mas des Chats. Accustomed to his right for food he felt secure —and with his sense of security came a sense that he owned the territory. He became dangerous.

For some time he was the central character at Mas des Chats. He dominated the scene because of his violent aggression, his passionate jealousy, his possessiveness. He made life wretched for the other cats, although Bruno bravely stood up to him, snarling and spitting, trying to challenge Nero until he was forced to retreat under tables and chairs. Nero had no scruples or restraint in his attacks. I tried every possible tactic—affection, support, anger, rejection. Nothing helped. Blanco fled, coming back only for hurried meals, often at dead of night.

Lily and Rosie retreated to the house, living mainly upstairs. Even there, they weren't safe. Nero leapt into the house through the cat window, and strode upstairs. The cats were terrified.

Rosie's face was stricken, her eyes wide with fear whenever she heard a small noise that might herald Nero's arrival.

She squeaked and cried reproachfully, making out that it was all my fault that they were living in a state of terror menaced by a monster.

Lily, even more frightened than Rosie, rushed from the house meowing pitifully.

She climbed trees and refused to come down.

In addition, she had to cope with Madame Malika's two small dogs, Violette and her daughter Caramel. They paid several visits every day to Mas des Chats, causing havoc by barking hysterically and chasing the cats. Once I found Rosie, Lily and Bruno sitting in a row on a branch of the mulberry tree. They peered nervously down at me through the thick leaves. They looked like the three monkeys, 'see no evil . . . hear no evil . . .'

They came down only after I reassured them that Violette and Caramel had departed.

Lily was particularly affected by all this mayhem. Her life became miserable and I felt angry and guilty.

I called on Madame Malika.

Symbolically speaking, she patted me patronisingly. She implied, pityingly, that I was a mad foreigner who had no idea how to treat animals. She made it clear she hadn't the faintest intention of taking care of or restraining the dogs—always pregnant or giving birth. She had, once before, made it equally clear that she'd take no notice of me when I went to see her about her cat Maurice, successor to the Siamese brothers. Maurice visited us for food. He'd had a severe infection of his eye and I went to Malika suggesting he should be seen by the vet. Malika disagreed. In the end, Maurice almost died, *had* to be taken to the vet and lost his eye.

'Why do you have animals?' I asked.

She shrugged. 'The children like them,' she said. So Caramel and Violette continued to rush, shrieking, through the garden and Nero to terrorise the cats.

Lily spent most of her time high in a cypress tree.

'Don't worry, Lily,' I said. 'I'll arrange things.'

I went to the vet to discuss Nero.

Castration, it was thought, might help. But there was no guarantee.

In desperation, I decided he must be castrated. Afterwards, he continued, for a while, as before. But he did change, slowly. I put this down to the fact that he began to feel cared for, loved, unthreatened. He lost his nervous anger, his fierce need to fight for survival. He became gentle. He accepted the other cats; they grew used to him. He was a fine, calm, dignified cat, very affectionate. His dark coat gleamed. He stared, with his golden eyes. He leapt like a miniature panther, playing games. Bruno began to dominate him but as a friend. They were, in fact, good friends and brothers in arms when necessary.

As for the dogs, for the time being I made a contract with the two of them. If I gave them a meal each morning, they agreed to go back home. That is to say, Violette agreed. Caramel, I later discovered, returned, smiling placatingly, by a circuitous route. She then lay hidden in the bushes for the rest of the day.

But as long as she didn't harass Lily or the other cats, that was allowed.

9

—◇—

Spring turned quickly to summer, warm nights and long days, a stillness of the air and a rapid ripening of corn and fruit—and as the
summer drifted slowly towards a mellow autumn, the two young cats
grew steadily into strong adults. Bruno became larger and more muscu-
lar than Blanco, who continued to be a little fragile—but perhaps it
was a fragility of the spirit rather than the body. He and Bruno
remained friends but were less dependent on one another.

Rosie began to feel affection for Bruno and he was infatuated with
her.

'But she's old enough to be your mother—or grandmother, Bruno,'
I said.

But Bruno didn't agree with me. He adored Rosie and admired
every aspect of her. Rosie *was* beautiful and she had a very graceful
walk, like a ballet dancer. Her ears were large and splendid and she
had a charming voice. Bruno, having gained her acceptance of him,
sometimes licked her lavishly. She seemed to enjoy that and nuzzled
into his coat, inviting him to further caresses. At other times he took
the rôle of dominating male, leaping on her and doing his best to
subdue unsubduable Rosie.

She was cross. She made it clear to Bruno that this was neither the
time nor the place. And she fussily smoothed her ruffled coat into
order, sending him packing.

But if Rosie was unsubduable, so also was Bruno. Larger than life,
in spirit, in the intensity with which he experienced the world, Bruno
began to establish himself as the chief cat of the household. Blanco,
on the other hand, continued to be shy and retiring, a sad little cat
with tragic eyes, very meek and well behaved, but fearful. While Bruno
was unafraid, or courageously held his ground, Blanco would hide if
threatened and run off into the fields, as when he was terrorised by
Nero.

Blanco couldn't bring himself to stand up to Nero's attacks as Bruno
tried to do and as Rosie did. Instead, he fled. Sometimes I looked for
him, but I never discovered where he went.

At times Bruno took the rôle of dominating male, leaping on her and doing his best to subdue unsubduable Rosie.

10

Rosie and I were sitting together in autumn sunlight in a brief pause in the morning's activities when two small black and white cats emerged together from a row of lavender bushes. Rosie, who had her eyes half shut in blissful dreams, immediately sat up, bristling. She was about to make a dash in their direction with the intention of hounding them off the premises, when I restrained her.

'Dear Rosie,' I said, 'do leave them alone for once.'

Rosie glared at me—a glare which made no secret of her feelings. The little black and white cats, mother and child, were new members of the cat group, who had appeared not long before at Mas des Chats. Rosie had despised them from the start. When would I learn not to take on riff-raff—raggle-taggle nobodies who were mere interlopers? Please allow her to get rid of an ignorant and ill-educated couple with whom she had nothing in common and whose country manners she wasn't prepared to tolerate. I tried to persuade her to change her views. Maman and Baby were sweet and natural, I told her, perhaps not highly sophisticated, not as cultured as Rosie was herself, but given a chance, and some contact with the select and brilliant group of cats already established at Mas des Chats, there was a good prospect of them improving themselves.

But Rosie refused to listen to me.

Maman and Baby were unscrupulous adventurers trying to muscle in on other people's property—and of a calibre so infinitely inferior to Rosie's own that she regarded them as beneath contempt.

'But Rosie,' I said, 'there'll be no one round here of anything like your quality, you are unique . . .' and I tickled her gently under her chin.

That was what she really wanted to hear. She was pleased. She sidled up against me and began to purr. I picked her up and held her close. She put her head under the crook of my arm and, still purring, let me know that she was very fond of me, very fond indeed. If she sometimes seemed critical . . .

'That's all right, dear Rose,' I said, 'I understand. I love you very

'There will be no one round here of anything like your quality,' I told her. 'You are unique.'
That was what she really wanted to hear.

much! But I'd greatly appreciate a little tolerance, a little
compassion . . .'

Maman had first appeared when Nero was at his worst, his moods
changing from savagery to indifference towards the other cats. She
arrived at dusk each day, a small black and white cat. I thought she
was a kitten, she was so little and round. She was painfully hungry. If

Nero was around, it was impossible to feed her. He fell on her with particular violence. If he was out of sight, she ate the food I gave her very quickly and drank a great bowl of milk before hurrying away. If Nero appeared and attacked her she'd fly off, screaming, into the fields, he pursuing her. Once, her shrieking went on for so long, I thought he was murdering her. I rushed off to try to find them. Before I could locate them, the screaming stopped. She was either dead or had escaped, or, perhaps, at worst, was badly wounded. In the morning I searched in the fields, but there was no sign of her. I was relieved, a day or two later, to see her, creeping through the dark, coming, again, for food. She had a deep triangular wound on her nose which left a permanent scar. But her need for food was great, and so was her courage. She'd come back determinedly in spite of the danger.

Later, I discovered she wasn't a kitten, just a very small cat. She was, in fact, quite old, although still young enough to give birth. She was the mother of a kitten who had almost identical colouring of coat. When her child was old enough, Maman brought her along with her and they fed together. By that time, Nero was tamer. The reign of terror was more or less over.

Marcelle, the *femme de ménage* who lived in the same area, said, when she saw Maman, 'I know that cat. It belonged to old Madame Bertini. She had ten cats. That's one of them, I'm sure.'

'Who's Madame Bertini?'

'She's dead. She died about six months ago. Then her husband died three weeks later. The district nurse found him unconscious on the floor. He died in hospital the same day.

'They lived in that house just behind ours. Her son lives there now.'

'What became of the other cats?'

Marcelle shrugged. 'Her daughter-in-law wouldn't want them— that's for sure.'

The Bertini house was just over the hill from mine.

I drove round to see the son and his wife in the hope they'd take the cats back.

Workmen were pulling the place to pieces and putting it together again. A short, dark woman, who must have been the Bertini daughter-in-law, was supervising them.

Maman was a marvellous mother, patient, caring, strong. She continued to look after Baby for years.

I spoke to her.

'Cats!' she said sharply. 'There are no cats here. Nobody here owns any cats. No—No—No . . .'

I put Maman and Baby in one of the outside rooms and gave them a basket each. But they didn't need two baskets, they shared one. Maman was a marvellous mother, patient, caring, strong. She continued to look after Baby for years. Baby, in return, loved her mother dearly. Maman was touchingly affectionate to her child, but if she thought Baby needed it she'd dole out a smart smack of a paw. Baby always allowed her mother to eat first before taking food herself (I've seen Maman give Baby a sharp cuff if the child took some titbit that she wanted to eat herself).

But Baby didn't become dependent on her mother. She had a life of her own—a tough, independent and courageous little cat, round and small like her mother and just as brave a survivor. She'd learned from her mother, however, to be tactful and gentle, firm but unobtrusive.

Of all the new immigrants, Maman made a point of keeping herself to herself and trying to persuade her daughter to do likewise. Young Baby was of course a little excitable and adventurous—children often were, as Maman knew only too well. She was wonderfully tolerant and patient with Baby but, nevertheless, a firm disciplinarian when necessary, and Baby obeyed her mother and followed her example. Maman instructed her to be as self-effacing as possible and to keep out of people's way. That strategy undoubtedly helped them to be accepted into the group without very many arguments. Scrupulously clean, gentle and calm, Maman let me know that she understood her place in the household and that although she had her own opinions, she saw no need to broadcast them. She could be firm and determined, however, when she chose. To prove this point she declined the plate of liver which I was putting before her—a little off, she thought— might she instead have a portion of mince?

Maman managed never to intrude on the other cats. Even after she and Baby had left the outside room and come to live modestly in the main part of the house, she never trespassed, never exceeded her territorial boundaries. Her place was in the downstairs rooms. Only once I saw her give way to a sudden uncontrollable curiosity. She trotted upstairs on her tiny misshapen legs and had a very good look and sniff as she sallied around each and every room. She reminded me of my German-Swiss grandmother, who would say, genially and with educated curiosity, when receiving new information:

'Ah ha! . . . Ach so! . . . *Eben!* . . . *Selbstverständlich!*'

Maman seemed to add exclamations of wonderment as she toured around. When she'd made a thorough inspection, she returned downstairs where she remained and didn't mention the matter again.

Baby, however, often raced upstairs and found little likely places to sleep, on small mats, in an unused basket, on the clean but unironed laundry (which all the cats loved to use as a bed) on a chair beside a radiator.

Baby had the same good qualities as her mother and the same round body, but she was well formed with straight limbs and spine. She had none of the bone defects of poverty and early inadequate feeding which Maman showed. Sleek and shining, Baby had extraordinary tilted green eyes with huge black oval pupils.

She was marvellously athletic. Up and down trees flew Baby, running like a leopard.

Maman, too, had green, green eyes with which she could give a hard, long stare when necessary.

Each was white coated with a saddle of black, a black-capped head and black legs. But while Maman's coat was shaggy and the white was ivory, Baby had smooth, brilliant fur and the white was true white.

'Baby?' said my sister Nora on hearing the name. 'Why just Baby?'

'Well—she's Maman's baby—but if Scott Fitzgerald can have a character called Baby, so can I.'

Baby knew her name and came when called. So, in fact, did all the cats. Maman and Baby had to be sterilised like all the other female cats, but when it was Baby's turn it was discovered she was pregnant. The father was Bruno.

Monsieur Lamartin, the vet, advised she should nevertheless have the operation.

'She's too young,' he said, 'to be a mother. It will exhaust her.'

After the surgery they lay together in their basket, comforting one another. But they recovered quickly.

When they first arrived, Maman and Baby used to go off each day, leaving in the morning and returning towards evening. Off they would go in tandem, over the hill, marching steadily. I concluded they must have gone to try to find their previous owner—or rather, Maman's owner, since Baby would have been too young to remember.

Maman had clearly been a loved cat. She sometimes had a sad expression. Once, when I saw her looking particularly lonely, I went to sit beside her where she lay. As I talked comfortingly to her, I suddenly remembered the French word *minou*, a term of endearment for a cat.

'*Minou!*' I said. '*Minou, minou!*'

Maman could hardly believe her ears. She had been lying with her back to me and now she rose and slowly turned. She stared at me with her green, green eyes.

'*Minou,*' I repeated, coaxingly.

'But you are not *her*,' said Maman's eyes.

Marcelle had told me that the old woman who had probably been Maman's owner had loved her cats.

'She'd go without food herself,' said Marcelle, 'so that the cats could eat.'

Maman, staring at me so fixedly and questioningly, had loved her mistress, had heard herself called *minou*, had been stroked and caressed by gentle, old hands. And I understood that Maman grieved, sad and bewildered at the loss of a lifelong friend. After a while, she gave up returning to her previous home. She remained at my house and made the best of things.

Mas des Chats: calm and peaceful, its small green garden sheltered by cypresses and shaded by great plane trees.

Lily was of legendary beauty, her soft, pure white coat shining silver in the sun.

A bossy, demanding, superb cat, Rosie took it for granted that she belonged to the élite.

Bruno, the cat who was to become the light of our lives.

His beauty was radiant, his personality captivating.

Solid, reassuring little Maman made a point of keeping herself to herself.

Her daughter Baby, almost a carbon copy of herself, had extraordinary tilted green eyes.

11

Not long after we'd settled in at Mas des Chats, a large, calf-size, black and tan dog came nosing round the house, very gently. Lily and Rosie screamed and rushed indoors. The dog stood and looked at me, questioning. Must he leave? Could he stay?

He had nothing against cats—he was at peace with cats. He'd noticed I put food out—for cats? For him? He hoped I knew that he was in the running for a dish of this or that if I could spare it. He was going now, but he hoped I'd remember. Very nice to have met me . . .

I discovered his name was Brilliant. He was my neighbours' dog, the Mabeilles, who lived near to Mas des Chats. The man was Giselle's brother—a slow, large, lazy man with the same confused blue eyes as his sister. His wife was very different. Thin, dark and energetic, she stormed through life, shouting! Her passion was music. She was learning to play the piano—a mature student. She was determined to succeed, although she'd no natural aptitude. Sometimes when I walked up on to the *colline*, past their house, I could hear her practising. Halting notes floated out over the feathery thyme and the wild lavender and the cistus.

Brilliant was really her dog—at least it was she who fed him and cared for him, such food and care as he received. I think she was fond of him but followed the peasant tradition in these parts over the treatment of animals—skimpy food and primitive medical care.

Brilliant and I, with the tacit agreement of the Mabeilles, established a relationship based on a meal a day. His dish was put out for him at the back of the house in the late afternoon when the cats were fed. Sometimes he turned up at odd times, especially at weekends and public holidays when the Mabeilles went out and left no food for him, expecting him to wait until they came back, often late at night. If I wasn't there he'd lie under the trees, front paws elegantly crossed, and wait patiently. Sometimes he missed the evening meal and turned up late at night. Once I went out in the moonlight to collect empty cat plates at the back of the house. I found Brilliant waiting there, hoping for food. He stood panting in the warm night air. He must have run

Whatever her private feelings, Lily pretended not to notice Brilliant and got on with normal living.

fast across the fields—great farm dog, smelling of sweat and earth, hungry. His coat shone in the silky light. Anxiously he waited.

I fetched food for him. He ate ravenously. Caramel came trotting round the corner of the house to find me and ran to Brilliant whom she loved. She reached up to him wagging her tail—and he wagging his. He was ten or eleven times her size.

She and I went back to the house while Brilliant finished his meal. I stayed for a while on the terrace, listening to the frogs shouting and looking at the moonlight on the garden.

Rosie and Lily, after they'd got over his size, became fond of him. Rosie even seemed quite affectionate and caring of him, once she'd got to know him.

I think Lily silently concurred but she pretended not to notice him and got on with normal living.

The other cats agreed with Rosie. Sometimes they'd come round with me to feed him and, if he was there, they stayed to watch him eat, thinking private thoughts, unhurriedly.

12

One afternoon I saw Violette and Caramel coming down the hill towards the bridge where sat a white and black cat with two small bundles of fur, one grey, one white. This was Hélène, a fairly recent arrival, with her two kittens.

Violette approached the bridge at a run and began barking bossily and noisily. Caramel took one look at the situation and made her way quickly across the canal at the back of the house.

Violette, galloping forwards, still barking, suddenly realised she'd have an eye scratched out if she came any nearer to Hélène. The white cat, rising to her feet and arching her back, was a terrifying sight. Violette skidded to a halt, looking foolish, her bark dying in her throat.

Hélène had made it clear that if Violette took one step nearer she'd be maimed for life and probably blinded into the bargain. And Hélène drew her stiletto.

Violette, foolish and confused, seemed baffled as to how to get down from the bank. Her daughter Caramel signalled that her best and safest plan was to go another way, round the back of the house.

But Violette still dithered, doing a kind of despairing dance on the edge of the bridge. Caramel, smiling amiably, decided she must go and fetch her mother and lead her to safety. This she did good-naturedly and cheerfully without making Violette feel a fool. They trotted home and Hélène with her two kittens remained in possession of the bridge. I admired her courage. She was a small and rather fragile cat—and Violette barking at full strength and charging with all her might was an alarming sight.

Hélène had first appeared some weeks earlier. I noticed her at dusk, on the bank at the back of the house. A ragged, bony white cat came fearfully out of the bushes to snatch a hurried meal from the cat bowl. She was dirty and wild. If she saw me she fled. I used to hide at the window and watch her thin face and ravenous eyes. I think she came from far away; the neighbours didn't know her when I asked. After she'd eaten well and regularly for a while she blossomed into a clean and handsome cat, young and spruce, bright white and black head and long, elegant black stockings. She must have given birth to her kittens on the wild hillside. There, in a deep, thorny hollow above the bridge, she nursed and reared them. I used to go up and look at the three of them among the ivy creepers and the stones. Hélène had a mysterious, pure serenity as a mother. The kittens felt perfectly protected. When they saw me on the ridge above their nest in the *garrigue*, they turned small blank, unafraid faces in my direction—three waifs in the jungle with the odds against them. The day she brought them down to the bridge was in preparation for a more permanent move.

When I understood she had a plan for the three of them to join the group at Mas des Chats, I spoke sternly to her.

'There are already six resident cats on the list here,' I said. 'Too many! There's no room for more.'

She received the news in silence.

'But,' I said, 'I am prepared to take on the three of you on a food-only basis.'

Still no murmur from Hélène. She had made her plans. Nothing would deflect her. She had found a place where there seemed to be a good food supply and nobody threw stones at her.

The result of her plans was that she and the kittens gradually established themselves in the small guest room which opened on to the terrace. It was the room which Maman and Baby had occupied early in their life at Mas des Chats. I felt forced to accept Hélène's decision.

The kittens grew quickly. Her grey-coated son became an elegant dandy, her white daughter, a replica of her mother. All three kept away from the other cats, going off for hours at a time to be in the fields.

Then, disturbingly, it became clear that Hélène was pregnant again. She must have conceived almost immediately after the kittens were born—not uncommon in cats. She had to be sterilised and the pregnancy terminated. There was no question of any more cats at Mas des Chats.

For this she had to be admitted to the house, enclosed in a quiet room the night before the operation and enclosed again for several days on her return from the clinic.

Hélène herself seemed calm and contented in her room. She allowed

Hélène seemed calm and contented in her room. She remained there peacefully for several days after her operation.

herself to be stroked. After her operation, she ate well and used her litter box as if she knew all about litter boxes. She purred. She was affectionate, demanding affection.

At one time in her life she must have been accustomed to people, had perhaps been cared for. What had happened, to turn her into a half wild, starving creature who chose to give birth to her young among the stones and bushes of the hillside?

She remained in her room, peacefully, the door shut.

Bruno lay outside, putting his inquisitive nose to the gap between door and floor.

What on earth, he wondered, was going on?

Meanwhile, Hélène's grey son looked everywhere for her. We later called him Oedipus because the tie between him and his mother was immensely strong. When she was away, recovering from the operation, he became desperately anxious. He rushed about looking confused and sad.

The daughter, Emilie, was less upset.

'Where is she?' Oedipus asked me again and again.

After some time, Hélène became restless. One morning I opened the door to let her out. She sallied cautiously to the threshold, peered out, skipped past the watchful Bruno, sidled to the wall and so went slowly down the stairs.

Oedipus found her on the terrace. He was ecstatic. He threw himself on her, clasping her and licking her. She in turn began licking him. They lay together for hours, endlessly caressing one another. Throughout their life at Mas des Chats, this ritual of loving took place again and again. If Oedipus went out hunting, the first thing he'd do on return was to find his mother, calling to her at the top of his voice. She would be as pleased as he when they met. She licked his head gently as he nuzzled her, and washed his coat all the way down to his tail as if he were still a kitten. But by now he was a tall, long, lithe young cat, whose grey coat fitted him closely like a body stocking. He had a large head with huge intelligent green eyes. Emilie was more independent—but she liked to be close to her mother at night.

All three still slept together in the outside room. I had insisted on this when Hélène had recovered from her operation.

Oedipus was by now a tall, lithe young cat, whose grey coat fitted him closely like a body stocking.

Then, dramatic events caused her to remove herself and her children from that room.

The drama was created by one of the cats which belonged to the sad Mlle Mabeille. Giselle had many cats. She never prevented them conceiving and although she drowned most of their kittens, one or two were always saved. She was fond of her cats but she hardly fed them. Most of them found their way to Mas des Chats and were fed by me. They were often injured or ill. But Mlle Mabeille was too confused herself to do anything to help them.

She was very pleased that I fed them. She knew they came to me and she saw them change from near skeletons to normal cats. She hadn't the means, she told me, to feed them herself. But her meanness was part of her madness. One cat was particularly disturbing. She was an elderly female who had been attacked by a dog. She had a deep, permanently open wound from which escaped terrible purulent discharge. She survived, mysteriously, and was even ravenously hungry. She, too, came across from Giselle's house to mine and ate from the food I put out. Then she began to oust Hélène from the little bedroom.

At first I couldn't understand Hélène's distress and why she and her children no longer slept in the bedroom but lay about among the lavender bushes. When I tried to coax Hélène back to her room, she cried and protested. Then I became aware of the sweet, stinking smell of illness and decay which Giselle's cat brought with her.

There, under the bed, was the old cat, snarling and spitting at me.

In the end, even Mlle Mabeille recognised that the old cat should be mercifully killed. This was done without, I believe, her suffering. But before this happened, Hélène and her young had become members of the household. She had found her way to a cupboard in the sitting-room. There she established herself, huddled together with her now large children, all three gazing at me in timid defiance when I discovered them.

Hélène's daughter, Emilie, also had to be sterilised—a traumatic experience for both of us. When she was old enough, I shut all doors and windows in the house and began to track her down. She tried frenziedly to escape. But it was essential to have the operation performed on the day arranged.

In the end I caught her and imprisoned her in a basket. She lay so still on the journey to the clinic, I thought she'd had a heart attack—but she'd perhaps fainted. After the operation I put her in an upstairs room, to recover gradually.

A day or two later she escaped, climbing from the high window down two stories of sheer wall.

She survived well, however, at that time. She would never let me come near her and for years she wouldn't go into the house, but she ate the hearty meals I put out for her whenever I saw her. She spent hours and days playing or hunting in the fields around the house. Sometimes she came twice a day for food; sometimes I didn't see her for a few days. Although often alone, she made a few friends among the other cats who came to eat, notably a large ginger tom. Lily rather fancied this ginger cat, and detested Emilie. Rosie and also Baby tried to chase Emilie away, but although she sometimes shrieked at the top of a raucous voice when they went after her, she came to no harm.

If Hélène was in the house and heard either of her children cry, she would come out to assess the situation. If she thought they needed protection she'd help them. But if she thought they were coping by themselves, she left them to it. I felt guilty and sad about Emilie's exile.

In general, Hélène and Oedipus integrated with the other cats without much difficulty. Just as Maman and Baby tried to keep out of the way of the established cats, so Hélène and Oedipus remained a little apart until they felt they were accepted.

And just as Maman had made one daring expedition upstairs, so, one night did Hélène. But she was infinitely stronger and braver than Maman had been. Hélène came onto and into the bed when I was asleep, bypassing Bruno who could hardly believe his eyes.

Purring profoundly, she snuggled beside me. There she spent the rest of the night. Dimly, in my sleep, I heard her purr. That was her one adventure. It was not repeated.

13

Caramel had always had her eye on Mas des Chats, it seems, almost from the moment she was weaned. Her mother, Violette, had been brought from Spain by the neighbour, José, consort of Malika, when he left his wife in Seville and moved north to France. She was a small barrel-shaped dog, ochre coloured, with a rather flat nose and black protruding eyes. She was not beautiful and she was very noisy. Her IQ was low. All in all, she wasn't an attractive dog. Her daughter was fathered by Dick, Monsieur Corbet's dog. Dick had great charm and a happy nature. Caramel inherited his charm and she was much prettier than her mother. She was the size of a large cat, her coat the colour of desert sand, lion coloured. She had a pleasant, intelligent face and a circular tail. Her legs were small and fragile but she could trot along briskly, at least as a rule. Once, when she had a spell of severe lameness, she was X-rayed at the veterinary clinic. The pictures showed that her bones were like the bones of an aged dog because she hadn't had proper food as a puppy. They had never properly calcified. In addition, a small bullet was lodged under the skin of her back. José used to fire his gun at random when he lost his Spanish temper.

Caramel had continued to break her side of the contract that I had made with her and Violette. She used to emerge from the bushes during the day if she thought she could get away with it, but she was intelligent enough to keep out of sight if she felt the moment was wrong. Both she and her mother were treated by Malika as if they were village dogs in the deep Sahara. They roamed wild, they ate what they could pick up. They were never allowed indoors—in fact, they had hardly any shelter even in the roughest weather. And they had never been house trained.

One day, Violette died. She had given birth, yet again, to four puppies. Three had already been given to friends. The fourth wandered around with Violette and Caramel as they scoured the neighbouring fields. If I saw him, I took him home to Malika, who looked at me accusingly as if it was my fault he'd strayed. Then she managed to get him adopted. Not long afterwards, Violette was discovered

On the death of her mother Caramel decided to take up official and permanent residence at Mas des Chats.

dead, one early morning. According to Malika, it was her heart. But there were a dozen other possible causes. She might have been ill for days without Malika noticing. At this point Caramel decided to take up official and permanent residence at Mas des Chats. Malika only noticed her absence a month later. By then Caramel had had her ovaries removed by the vet, Monsieur Lamartin. She had already had at least two litters. Now there were too many animals at Mas des Chats.

Malika, when one day she happened to see Caramel in the road, suddenly noticed the scars of the operation. She marched over to see me with her latest baby in her arms.

She had an angry outburst.

'Why didn't you ask me before Caramel had her operation? You should have asked me!'

I was taken aback.

I said I was truly sorry I'd upset her. I said I thought she'd abandoned Caramel and had no further interest in her.

'You think of us like *merde!*' Malika shouted bitterly. 'You should have asked me!'

I was distressed. Malika was right. She and her family were deplored and despised by the people of the neighbourhood, including me. They lived like the very poor and the very primitive in any country—rubbish thrown anywhere and everywhere, too many children whom they couldn't look after properly, children howling, someone always unemployed yet four second-hand cars always tearing up and down the lane. One of her daughters, under age, was often brought home by the police, appeared in juvenile courts, was sent to reform schools, reappeared and was in trouble again. José had a hot temper, Malika and he quarrelled violently. But she wasn't a bad woman and she had a kind heart.

When she shouted at me over Caramel, the child in her arms began to cry.

I said, 'Oh dear! Oh dear! I'm so sorry . . .'

At which Malika gave a strange little shy smile and said, 'She's hungry,' and jogged the baby up and down.

I said, 'I'm truly sorry I upset you about Caramel. I really thought you'd given her up.'

Malika said, 'The matter is now closed,' and she marched back home.

'Don't you want to take Caramel with you?' I called.

61

She shouted, over her shoulder, 'I expect she'll come back every now and then,' and she and the child disappeared behind the laurel hedge.

By this time, Caramel had adamantly made up her mind never to return to her original home.

Then I remembered that, not very long before, Caramel had disappeared for three weeks, as reported to me by Mme Corbet. She had returned looking thin and dishevelled. She came first to Mas des Chats, where I was sitting by the swimming pool. I went over to give the news next door.

Only the eldest daughter was at home. 'Caramel's back,' I said.

A look of total disbelief crossed Rosa's face.

'She's back?' She looked astounded. I went home wondering if they'd tried deliberately to get rid of Caramel, given her to someone, dropped her out of the car far away, so astonished and dismayed had Rosa seemed.

I decided that Caramel should stay and we'd make the best of her at Mas des Chats.

It wasn't easy. Caramel was a very agitated and disturbed little creature. Frantically possessive and jealous, it was torture for her to see me giving any attention to the cats. I did my best to comfort and soothe her.

'We love you too,' I told her. 'Everybody can be loved. There's love for all.'

She very gradually became a little reassured. I decided to take her on a daily walk which she grew to love. We usually walked each morning. Caramel knew when the outing was imminent and became wildly excited.

We drove to some beautiful places—the mountain tops or the high mountain paths, the borders of the canals, little roads in the flat valley between the Alpilles and Avignon. We walked in all weathers. In winter, ice lay on the floor of the canals where the water had been drained and the Mistral flailed us like a whip. In the spring there were a thousand wild flowers and nightingales sang from every bush.

In the high hills, above the pine woods, there were vast views of valleys and gorges, great rocky outcrops and vertical cliffs and, far

We went for walks along the borders of canals, and the little roads in the flat valley between the Alpilles and Avignon.

away to the south, beyond the plain, the silvery shine of the sea. In the summer there were the flowers of gorse and thyme and rosemary, and humming bees gathering honey, and mountain air.

Sometimes it seemed as if we had all the stony roads of the Alpilles to ourselves—and usually the grass-covered banks of the canals were deserted. On the banks grew wild orchis and the little brown bee orchis and buttercups and kingcups in a blaze of yellow. Everywhere the brilliant light of Provence made colours crystalline and outlines razor sharp.

Not far from the Mas des Chats the canal descended from the hills, in a series of splendid waterfalls. When the canal water was flowing at full capacity, it fell heavily, like a solid curtain, to crash in a pool below among the débris of our civilisation—plastic bottles, pieces of broken polystyrene, tins, rags, the froth and foam of detergents, old shoes, insecticide containers, rotting cigarette boxes.

All around were the silent and sensitive Mediterranean pines, tactfully ignoring the rubbish. Caramel and I tried to do the same.

14

'A cherry tree! You need a cherry tree! You must have a cherry tree
and it must be near the house. Then all you have to do is take a few
steps to pick the cherries and eat them immediately. Early in the
morning, when it's fresh and cool. I have a cherry tree next to my
house. Before I'm dressed in the morning I go out and gather a few
cherries and eat them straight away. Nothing more agreeable . . .'

Monsieur Lamartin, the veterinary surgeon, gave me this good
advice as he stood on the terrace of Mas des Chats. He'd come to see
one of the cats who was ill and, on leaving, he'd stopped for a moment
to look with approval at the garden bright with spring bloom and
young leaves. He'd noticed that a cherry tree was lacking.

In due course I followed his advice and Monsieur Mercier the gardener planted a cherry tree in the grass on the edge of the terrace.

Shortly after arriving at Mas des Chats I'd been very relieved to find
an extremely efficient veterinary clinic on the outskirts of the little
nearby market town.

It was owned and run by Monsieur Lamartin—or rather Docteur
Lamartin—an elegant, fastidious man in his middle age. He took great
pride in his immaculate clinic and a good deal of the money earned
in the practice went back, after the expenses had been paid, into
improvements and additions made to the building.

A man who became a friend of mine, a well-known painter, fed and
cared for twenty or more cats and various dogs in the small village
where he lived. He often was in need of Docteur Lamartin's services
and he told me once he believed it was he who'd paid for the new
plate glass door at the clinic entrance. I, with my ten cats and their
considerable medical expenses, believed I'd made a fair contribution
to the construction of a new operating theatre. The fees at the clinic
were on the high side, but it seemed that those who really looked
after their animals could afford them. The waiting room was usually
crowded (there was a very large number of huge mild-tempered dogs
and their owners whenever I went there).

There were four assistant vets younger than Dr Lamartin and they could well have done with another one. I often waited a long time with cat or dog patient before being summoned into one of the clean, austere consulting rooms. Dr Lamartin made even the gardener wear a white coat.

In spite of the pressure of work, Dr Lamartin and his colleagues took their time over each case, listening, unhurriedly, to the owner's story, enquiring, examining, advising, prescribing and chatting. I was always surprised at their compassion and how patient and gentle they were with both animals and owners, no matter how demanding and trying.

Was this, I wondered, the result of their training or a characteristic of the French people? The doctors behaved similarly with their human patients, I'd noticed. Everyone, however humble, seemed to know what his blood pressure was and should have been and the level of his serum cholesterol—together, very often, with a good deal of other personal medical information. The patient's wish to know and understand was respected.

Dr Lamartin had had a computer installed in the clinic to keep the medical records of every patient. When it came to my cats, the vet often had to run through the whole list of them before arriving at the relevant one in trouble. I was fascinated to see their names, illnesses and treatments appear on the screen one after another—Rosie, Lily, Bruno, Neron, Fleur and Charlotte (Maman's and Baby's official names thought up on the spur of the moment), Monsieur le Gris, Hélène, Oedipus and Katy. Each one had had some problem at one time or another.

Dr Lamartin was an interesting and unusual man. He was an excellent surgeon and genuinely fond of the animals he treated. He was a talented painter, self-taught. He loved the countryside across which he rode on a fine black horse looking dashing in impeccable habit. I could well imagine him gathering cherries in a silk dressing-gown and leather slippers, in the first pale sunshine of a summer's day. He was kind and considerate. He—or one of the junior partners—never failed to turn up at Mas des Chats at the hour arranged when one of the cats was really ill.

One afternoon, in the season when cherries were ripe, he and his wife appeared unexpectedly at Mas des Chats with a large basket of their own delicious freshly-picked cherries. The cats heartily disliked medical treatment, except for Bruno and Rosie; they all disappeared, if they could, the moment they heard the sound of Dr Lamartin's car. The ill cats had to be imprisoned if he was expected, nervously waiting for what seemed to them a terrifying ordeal.

He once came to vaccinate all ten of them and that was an ordeal for all of us. He had bought and brought with him a huge butterfly net with which to trap and hold recalcitrant cats. Lily was caught in this under one of the old olive trees, to her immense indignation—a very large butterfly indeed.

Dr Lamartin was pleased with the success of this trap and vaccinated Lily through the netting. It took her hours to get over the experience. She cleaned and recleaned every hair on her coat, muttering to herself dementedly. But in the end she settled down and was able to take a light supper.

After the upheavals caused by this mass vaccination I was, the following year, allowed to fetch the vaccine from the clinic. I could then vaccinate each cat quietly at an opportune moment. Each cat was given a pretty little book at the clinic in which name, medical treatment and vaccinations were inscribed.

My taking the vaccine home was a special privilege, permitted only because of my medical training.

I learned how to give cats injections but I always found this a nerve-racking business. Like most other cats, eight out of my ten resisted treatment vigorously.

Rosie and Bruno were the exceptions. Rosie accepted some of the benefits of living in the twentieth century. Bruno, as always, trustingly believed that what I did for him was bound to be for the best.

15

I was lucky to have found, after a few trials and errors, an excellent *femme de ménage* and a gardener.

The *femme de ménage*, Marcelle, was a charming, generous woman, fiftyish perhaps, her age hard to tell, so quick and vigorous she was, so young in movement. She was plump, rosy and blue-eyed and she liked bright colours and closely fitting clothes. She lived with a young raw Moroccan, Ali, who came from a remote village in the Atlas Mountains.

She'd met Ali when working in the orchards in the cherry-picking season. For him, she'd recklessly abandoned her French husband Marc and eloped. Marc was older than she was, dour, coarse and unkind. He never forgave Marcelle and lived in bitterness. The people of the community also found it hard to forgive her and sometimes people spat at her in the streets of the little town and insulted her. Even Monsieur Corbet, usually so tolerant and intelligent, said to me, shaking his head in condemnation,

'She left her husband, a good Frenchman, for an ARAB!!'

But Marcelle, who had a streak of wildness in her, stuck to Ali and made a success of her life with him. She felt stimulated in the company of his friends, all Moroccans, lively and noisy in contrast to the local farmers, whom she found dull.

The cats liked her and she loved them.

Sometimes I heard her talking to Lily who nervously tolerated her.

'Leelee!' she cooed in a sweet high-pitched voice. 'Leelee!' And she put out a small, round, work-roughened hand to stroke Lily's beautiful white coat.

There came a time when she was forced to leave the little house near mine where she and Ali lived, and move to the town. She was terribly apprehensive. She'd lived in the *quartier* all her life and had never travelled more than fifty miles away from it.

'Marcelle,' I said to comfort her, 'where you're going is only five kilometres away. Look at me, I've moved all the way from England!'

She looked at me in sudden compassion, tears in her eyes.

One of Lily's favourite occupations was sniffing flowers.

'Yes, of course,' she said, 'you also are uprooted, *déracinée*, like me . . .' and she sighed at our mutual plight.

But after she'd made the move she settled contentedly into her new town lodging and was happy there.

She continued to work for me for a year or two. She travelled from the town centre to Mas des Chats on her motor scooter, known in these parts as a *mobilette*.

The *mobilette* was dangerous to ride in high winds and rain, but Marcelle insisted on making the journey in all weathers. Blown by the Mistral, soaking from the rain, she arrived punctually, pink-cheeked, blue eyes sparkling, undeterred. She then removed layer after astonishing layer of protective clothing and emerged a plump, short, middle-aged, pretty little woman in a freshly ironed apron—her feet bare. At once she set to and began to wash the tiled floors.

But after a while she grew tired of making the journey. She went, instead, to work with Ali who now had a market stall where he sold fruit and vegetables on market days in all the little towns of the Alp-illes. Marcelle enjoyed the social life of the markets. She was not embarrassed at being exposed to angry and contemptuous looks and comments as Ali's woman. But eventually, as Ali made a better living, she gave up work altogether. She acquired a small, blue-eyed, many-coloured cat and together they stayed comfortably at home.

I had to find a substitute for Marcelle. This wasn't easy, but after some trials and failures I found Madame Mauron, a neat, blonde, attractive woman who had come from the north of France with her husband because his employers had transferred him. He worked as an engineer in one of the great aircraft factories on the coast. Madame Mauron had been a secretary in a small office in Lille. She found it impossible to obtain similar work in the little nearby towns. Needing to earn money, she became a *femme de ménage* to a few families (friends of mine) in the neighbourhood of Mas des Chats. We all agreed she wasn't really suited to the physically demanding cleaning required of her in the large old farmhouses. But she worked hard and conscientiously in her limited way.

She arrived punctually on her appointed days, fashionably dressed and driving a small smart car. She would change her shoes, put on her spectacles and work in silent concentration. I never learned what she was really thinking or feeling. Was she angry? Was she resentful? Formally polite and formally smiling, Madame Mauron was a mystery to all her clients and she clearly wished to remain mysterious—or at least to preserve her enigmatic mask. There were moments when I felt she looked on me almost as a mentally defective child—or, at best, an odd foreigner whose eccentricities she tolerated because she must.

There were times when I thought we made brief contact.

But I accepted her reserve and in all the years she worked for me, I never discovered her true identity—nor her first name.

Monsieur Mercier the gardener was a strong, vigorous man who ran rather than walked and never stopped to rest. There was a nervous violence in the depths of him, only rarely expressed outwardly. He had been unhappy as a child. His parents were divorced and, an only child, he had been made to live with his complaining, difficult mother. His father had remarried and was a tenant farmer of Mabeille *père*, father of Giselle. He had visited his father at weekends—and there fallen in love with the pretty and privileged Giselle. He'd adored her —at a distance—as a boy. She probably never knew and was hardly aware of him. The anger which simmered in him was perhaps the result of these childhood experiences.

He loved the garden and he loved the plants and flowers and animals and he was full of love for his children and grandchildren. This love was overwhelmingly greater than his anger.

One day, when he was working in the garden, Giselle Mabeille chose to pay one of her visits to me. Monsieur Mercier stood and stared at her. She went up to him and looked at him with dazed blue eyes.

'Do I know you?' she asked.

'I don't know if you know *me*,' he said, 'but I know *you*.'

At this she laughed nervously. He gave her his name and his father's name.

She seemed dimly to remember. A few more questions—then she drifted away, laughing, as she must always have done, leaving him troubled.

He turned to me.

'She used to be very beautiful,' he said, 'it's sad to see her now . . . but she was always a little . . . confused, a little . . . mad . . .'

Not long afterwards Giselle, her illness worse, was put into the clinic St Paul, where Van Gogh had been a patient. She stayed there for some time. When she was released and returned home, she no longer wandered round the countryside. We saw no more of her.

Only her hungry cats came to me to find food.

71

16

How to describe the magic of Bruno? First, his looks, his beauty and the goodness and calm of his intelligent face; his trustingness, his gentleness, his friendship, his endearing squint. In the night I was sometimes woken by a feather-light touch on the tip of my nose, my lips, my eyelids. He was signalling to me with a perfectly co-ordinated, perfectly controlled paw to invite him into the bed in wintry weather so that he could warm himself against the warmth of my body. Sometimes he came to lie on the pillows beside my head, positioning himself so deftly and silently I only knew he was there when I woke in the morning.

He had all the qualities we think of as virtues—tact, sensitivity, tolerance, generosity, good humour. There was no malice in him, no bitterness. He was only angry when he was defending his territory and when he was keeping Monsieur le Gris in check—that's to say, when he needed to show that he was the top cat, the master of Mas des Chats.

Rosie and Lily used to make out he had been a farmer's boy, a rude peasant, when he first arrived. They'd civilised him, they insisted, Rosie with her sophisticated British know-how, Lily with her ladylike manners. In my view, he was a natural gentleman, a born aristocrat. Rosie would say maybe, but he still had a lot to learn, when he first arrived. Learn he did, and he became a much loved character. An urbane host to my friends (he'd do a round of the guests in the salon with a few polite words to each), he was also court jester, clown, show-off, star. He had a repertoire of comic tricks to amuse the other cats. His and their favourite was 'The Dancing Carpet'. Bruno would raise the corner of a light rug by butting against it with his nose or scooping it up with his paw. Once the corner was lifted he'd dive under the rug so that it covered him completely. He'd then begin to waltz around the room—usually the kitchen. Being invisible, he'd managed to create the illusion that the rug was dancing of its own accord. The other cats would sit around watching, fascinated.

'Roll up! Roll up!' Bruno seemed to signal to the other cats, like a fairground showman, urging them to come and see the Dancing Rug, fun guaranteed or your money back.

The beautiful cats sat staring, spellbound. When Bruno was tired of the game and crawled out again from under the rug the other cats would go stealthily towards it and examine it cautiously, trying to discover the cause of its magical powers. A few of them tried to imitate Bruno, notably Baby, but they never quite succeeded.

He often liked to lie and sleep tucked under a rug or carpet. Sometimes he rushed at the carpet edge like a bull charging a matador and, tossing a corner in the air, he clambered under it. Sometimes, the fringe of the mat lay across his forehead, giving him the look of an Eastern king or a lady of the harem.

He found large paper bags—the hypermarket frozen-food bags—irresistible, if they were lying on the kitchen floor. He'd dive inside them, then rustle them provocatively, inviting the attention of the other cats. If one approached, out shot a long paw which delivered a slap. That was the signal for a wild game to begin.

He liked also to be wrapped in coats, curtains, dressing-gowns—whatever happened to be handy. Sometimes he'd pull down sheets stretched across a metal drying rack, tumble them into a comfortable hooded nest and go to sleep in them. Once, when my back was turned for ten seconds, he managed to get into the electric clothes-drying machine just before it was switched on, filled with damp towels and pillow slips. The drum rotated a couple of turns before I cut the power, alarmed by the loud thumping noise. Opening the door of the machine I found, to my horror, Bruno completely enfolded in damp linen. He came out looking a little dazed but was unharmed.

Undaunted by his experience he did attempt to try it again at other times but I was obsessionally careful about looking in the machines before I put them in action.

Soft, silky and supple, he could slide into narrow recesses. Once he slipped unnoticed into the space between the glass doors and the wooden shutters just as I was locking up before leaving on a two-day journey. Some mysterious telepathy, some vibration of the bond which linked us, made me go back and open the door. Bruno, looking sheepish, was thankful to be let out.

Bruno liked to wrap himself in coats, curtains, sheets—whatever happened to be handy to make into a comfortable hooded nest.

He seemed a little reproachful that I'd been so slow in coming to release him. He'd found it rather stuffy, I gathered.

All the females of the cat group loved him—even, I think, Lily. They postured and cooed before him and he was kind and affectionate in return.

Baby was crazy about him. She squeaked ecstatically as soon as she saw him, even at a distance. She rubbed her little round body against

All the females of the cat group adored him, but Rosie was his great love.

him and thrust herself under his nose from head to tail, unashamed and immodest. He took this good-naturedly, giving her a little hug and pinching her bottom to humour her—but if she overdid it he lost patience and moved away. Rosie was his great love and usually played 'hard to get'.

Bruno, as leader, seemed to hold the cat community together. With his intense personality he created tension—and it was this that drew the cats into a coherent group. He had positive and negative feelings towards each of them and they to him. Allies were Nero first and Oedipus second. Enemy was Monsieur le Gris. And the ladies were simply drawn towards him. Even Caramel, who was indifferent to the other cats of the household, respected and, I think, admired Bruno.

Lily remained aloof but wistful. Sometimes she too nudged the glorious Bruno, but although he gave her an occasional lick and a nose-to-nose greeting, he wasn't really interested in her. Rosie was the love of his life. Lily sighed. She pretended not to mind and began to focus on the lizards which appeared suddenly out of their niches in the old walls. I told her how beautiful she was. I told her she was my beautiful white cat from Hampshire. She sighed again. Sometimes she came to rub herself against my legs with a little squeak of friendship. But mostly she was alone, with her memories and dreams.

17

One bitter night in winter, Blanco vanished. I was used to his going away for many hours, sometimes a day or two at a time. But he'd come back for food, perhaps in the middle of the night. There were anxious times when, if I hadn't seen him for a very long period, I'd wait up for him. In the end he'd arrive, sliding silently through the open window like a little white ghost. He would look at me intently with his sad blue eyes asking for food. When I put down his plate he'd eat ravenously. Then he'd rest for a while before going off again. That night, he went away and never returned.

Snow fell, followed by heavy frost. In an anguish of anxiety at the possibility of his being trapped, perhaps injured, perhaps ill or poisoned, I searched for him. Round and round the frozen fields I went, calling, day after day. No sign, no sound.

Once, I thought I heard him cry—but then there was silence. The sound wasn't repeated.

After two weeks, I gave up searching. He had gone.

Many cats disappeared in those parts. Their lives were at risk if they went far from home. Even in the garden, they might have found and eaten a mouse or other small creature that had been poisoned.

Sometimes birds like crows or magpies let fall from their beaks as they flew pellets of poisoned food, which they'd picked up far away.

Huge amounts of poison which destroyed the blood cells were put down in the area. The communes and the farmers and others regularly made attempts to wipe out the wildlife. Traps also were laid. Cats and dogs sometimes died even if treated after absorbing some of those poisons. Anyone could buy lethal pesticides in the supermarket.

Poisoning wasn't the only cause of death among domestic animals. Hunters shot cats, at times—and cats were often crushed by cars driven at violent speeds along the narrow roads, especially at night. Several cats disappeared who were well known to me because they visited Mas des Chats regularly for food, among them a number belonging to Giselle Mabeille. Her cats were often injured, often ill, often in trouble. Anxious, sometimes tearful, she'd visit me to enquire if I'd seen them.

A notable character among these outside cats was Nelson, so called by me because one eye was blind, irreparably damaged by some injury. He came every day to eat. He never missed except once or twice when badly damaged. Even then, as soon as he could he dragged himself painfully along to have a meal.

I admired him for his courage and persistence. It was clear he was a cat who feared human beings and who must have been cruelly treated by them. He depended for food on stealing, begging or hunting. He seemed to me like a rascally old man with cloak and staff, such as might be seen in the marketplace of an Arab town calling, 'Alms! For the love of Allah! Alms!'

During the two years he came to Mas des Chats he suffered many more injuries to his poor body. Twice he had what looked like a broken paw.

It wasn't possible to approach Nelson, let alone examine and treat him. The paw mended each time on its own, miraculously it seemed.

Another time he had an injury to the skin of his head and face around his already damaged eye.

Then he vanished.

I knew after a few days when he didn't turn up to eat that I'd never see him again. He used to appear so regularly, trudging over the hill, and he was so dependent on the food he received that his absence meant something had happened to him. One day without seeing him meant he couldn't make the journey. He never came back.

I was sad for brave and battered Nelson. I felt he'd been finally cornered by someone who'd many times tried to destroy him. I went up across the hill to see if I could find him, perhaps injured or ill.

Up there, too near the house according to the law, was a ruffianly man with a dog and a gun. I asked had he seen one of my cats, white, with a blind eye.

Before the words were out of my mouth he said no, he'd seen no cats, no cats at all. I went on down the path to the little bridge, chilled, apprehensive. There was a sense in the air of evil, of brutality.

The lives of cats in the area seemed very fragile even though they were each supposed to have nine.

I feared for mine.

18

Spring returned, the second spring. Sometimes I talked to Rosie and Lily about old times.

'Now the snowdrops will be out,' I said. 'Do you remember them? That patch by the old wall—and those that came up in the grass near the orchard? It's spring in England, primroses next, and buds on the daffodils under the apple trees. Do you remember the woods and the foxes?'

Rosie looked at me steadily, making me painfully aware that it had been my decision to leave.

Rosie looked at me steadily, making me painfully aware that it had been my decision to leave England.

Lily was gentler. She listened ecstatically as I talked, reminding me how she used to float across the newly mown lawn like a plump summer cloud, a giant puffball; how she insisted on staying out in the rain, how she caught fieldmice on the edge of the cornfield.

Rosie continued to look at me—my English cat who could remember England and April in a Hampshire garden.

———————◇———————

In early summer, when the days were already hot, Caramel and I walked along waterways lined with trees which met in an arch high overhead, dappling the sunlight below. The birds still sang loudly.

The broom was in full flower, incandescent yellow, loading the air with heavy scent. There were fields of lavender-coloured companula, paling to porcelain mauve in the heat of the sun, and purple vetch and wild sweet peas and roses.

Caramel panted and walked slowly. I wore a straw hat and dark glasses. Near the road, we saw, here and there, the remains of the lunches of picnickers, the crunched shells of hard-boiled eggs, cigarette ends, plastic cups, empty bottles. Sometimes half-naked holiday-makers, skin well oiled, were stretched out in the sun on patches of grass among the olive trees and wild flowers.

They looked blissful.

19

Bruno's sudden raucous howl let me know that once again he'd discovered Monsieur le Gris lying on the bed in the main bedroom.

Bruno then made a determined and successful effort to turf Monsieur le Gris from his comfortable position on the pillows. He achieved this with the maximum of noise and drama, using his famous 'Ladies from Hell' howl, like that of the kilted Scots in World War I.

Monsieur le Gris grumbled and growled and cried. Bruno was merciless. If le Gris had not decided to retreat, Bruno would have jumped on him with his full and considerable weight. In order to avoid humiliation and flying fur Monsieur le Gris slunk sulkily away. Bruno shadowed him to make sure the upstart was safely out of the way.

If le Gris decided to stand up to Bruno—as he sometimes did—Bruno would punish him so that le Gris would have to run for shelter under a bed or chair until Bruno's temper cooled. For a while Bruno would lie waiting for him to emerge, then, bored, would go away.

Monsieur le Gris arrived one summer's day—a young rangy cat, grey and white like Oedipus. He was hungry and in bad condition, but he soon revived. His behaviour was aggressive and rough with the other cats who were nervous of him or irritated by him according to their nature. With me, he tried to be clumsily affectionate.

I find it hard to remember just how he became attached to the group.

By then, eight cats lived more or less comfortably together—Rosie and Lily, Bruno and Nero, Maman and Baby, Hélène and Oedipus.

It was during my second summer in Provence that Monsieur le Gris appeared.

It must have been the heat, causing laziness, the life out of doors, a careless inattention—suddenly I realised Monsieur le Gris belonged to Mas des Chats.

Bruno was the only cat who objected seriously. He was furious with Monsieur le Gris for daring to intrude—and even angrier when le Gris misguidedly tried to challenge him. He spent a great deal of time and effort keeping le Gris in his place. But Monsieur le Gris bounced up

Suddenly I realised that Monsieur le Gris belonged to Mas des Chats.

again each time he was put down. Boisterous, brave, eternally hopeful, he tried his luck time and again. He wasn't popular with any of the other cats, except Oedipus.

Rosie regarded him with contempt as a brutish peasant, badly mannered and gauche. In his awkward hurry to be accepted, Monsieur le Gris lunged out, pushed and butted and bit, in play I thought. He didn't understand how strong and heavy he was.

He became extremely large—not fat, but powerful. He was, poor fellow, destined always to be the number two.

He was a very jealous cat. All the cats were jealous of one another, especially when it came to stroking and caressing. Monsieur le Gris compensated for his feelings of inferiority by making it his business to oust every other cat from his or her chosen resting place. Of course, he couldn't do this with Bruno—nor with Nero. But all the other cats suffered from his pushing and jostling them where they lay until they felt bound to move.

But le Gris couldn't be in more than one place at a time, although he would have liked to take over all the beds at once.

When Oedipus could tear himself away from his mother, he let himself be licked and caressed by Monsieur le Gris.

After he felt settled, he did his best to defend the territory at Mas des Chats, fending off strange cats even when they were fiercer and tougher than he was.

He was castrated, like Bruno and Nero, to preserve his life—to prevent him from travelling on the dangerous roads at night. In spite of this, he went on bullying and harassing the younger cats, especially Katy who was terrified of him.

He fell in love with Oedipus—and Oedipus with him. When Oedipus could tear himself away from his mother, he let himself be licked and caressed by Monsieur le Gris. They were deeply attached to one another.

A baby at heart, needing endless reassurance and patient care, Monsieur le Gris pretended to himself that he was a hero. In his dreams, he was top cat, master of Mas des Chats.

20

Katy was the last, youngest and lightest cat to join the household. She was found as a tiny shivering kitten, in the courtyard of a block of flats in the town. It was January, bitterly cold, with the Mistral raging. Two English friends found her. They had an apartment at the top of the building. They saw her at dusk, crouching behind a bush, lost, they thought, ready to die of hunger and cold. They took her in. They enquired in the neighbourhood and put up notices in shops and doorways. No one, it seemed, had lost a kitten.

She lived for some time in the apartment. Black, with a white chest and belly and feet, she had an unusual head. Her face was very pointed, her forehead round, her large eyes a brilliant orange. She had, for a time, a lonely and difficult life, high up in the apartment overlooking the hills and the roofs of the little town. She was often left on her own for hours at a time. She had, of course, no mother from whom to learn, no other cat to help her recognise her own identity, her catness. She relied on her instincts, was clean and affectionate. She toured around the apartment, knocked ornaments off the mantelpiece, chased balls.

The friends had to return to England, and asked me if I would take her. One more cat to join the group—the last, I vowed. She had the greatest difficulty integrating with the other cats. All disliked her or, at least, rejected her, even hunted her. Extremely sensitive and completely lacking in confidence, Katy did not or could not fight back, could not stand up for herself. Instead, she fled.

Rosie was particularly opposed to her. Not only did she try to chase her away herself, she encouraged Bruno to do the same. One day I was in the bedroom with Rosie and Bruno when the hapless Katy put her nose in at the door. Rosie tensed and half rose up from where she lay on the bed. She glared at Katy. Then, I swear, I distinctly saw her pass a message to Bruno by some subtle means, telepathy, or gestures invisible to the human eye. The message read, 'You'd do me a good turn if you'd throw that creature out of our place,' rather as Henry II had cried out to his court, 'Will no one rid me of this turbulent priest?'

Amiable Bruno didn't at first respond—or rather, his initial response was of puzzlement. Who? Her? She's not a bad little thing really.

But Rosie, becoming angrier at Katy's continued intrusion, made her message urgent and finally incited Bruno to action.

And so he began to harass Katy. He shadowed her. Where she went, he followed. He lay down when she lay down and stared. The message and the menace were clear. Poor Katy, who had been fond of him like all the cats, began to be afraid of him.

Rosie was very pleased. She'd succeeded in getting him to carry out her plan of forcing Katy to leave the Mas.

I decided to have a talk with Rosie. She had, from her earliest days, always made it plain to me that she was a great believer in the rules of evolution as formulated by Darwin. The fittest and only the fittest should survive. She regarded herself, of course, as belonging to the supremely fit, eminently suited to preserving the species in its most attractive form. To this end Rosie insisted she had to be allowed to

Rosie regarded herself, of course, as belonging to the supremely fit, eminently suited to preserving the species in its most attractive form.

respond to instinctive impulses. She was never tired of rubbing this in. Instincts had kept the cat species going for a few million years, why stop now?

She was simply following her instincts when she tried to chase from the premises Katy, Emilie and all the outside cats.

When I protested and tried to restrain her, she was indignant. She refused to co-operate with my ideas of a Utopian garden where cat loved cat and all was peace and tranquillity, and the leopard lay down with the lamb.

'There's enough food for all,' I tried to tell her.

But it wasn't just a matter of food, she proclaimed, it was a matter of territory, a question of numbers, an appropriate response to a fundamental drive.

'Leaving all that aside, Rosie,' I said, 'you'd oblige me if you were a bit nicer to Katy—and also to Monsieur le Gris.'

Rosie looked at me with her great eyes veiled, her thoughts unspoken but easy to guess.

'I'm trying to make a civilised community here,' I pleaded. 'Surely you can understand?'

She opened her eyes wide.

Her notions of civilisation didn't coincide with mine. She didn't consider it civilised to allow bigger, stronger, rougher, uglier cats to muscle in on her territory, to take away her livelihood and reduce her to a heap of shivering neurosis and to destroy the complex relationships that already existed. Since I seemed to fail so abysmally in keeping out unpleasing strangers, why not leave it to her?

I was reminded that years before, when Rosie was still a young, quite fragile cat, she had bravely defended the boundaries at Ashford.

There weren't many intruders in that lonely place, but once a cat from the top of the hangers had made her way down the hillside and had tried, not once, but many times, to take over the garden. This cat was much bigger and heavier than any of our cats. She was also very determined to establish herself as top cat.

Rosie, then only half grown, took on the difficult task of sending this cat packing. She eventually succeeded (where even I had failed) to the relief of us all.

I was determined to preserve Katy, most touching of little cats.

I thought often and seriously about Rosie and her views on the benefits of instinctive behaviour, the survival of those best equipped to survive.

Was I trying too hard to achieve an impossible task, preserving and comforting too many cats? Should I rather have followed the laws of evolution, let only the fittest survive? It wasn't in my nature and I was determined to preserve Katy—most touching of little cats. When she was hunted by other cats she disappeared. I searched everywhere. She was away sometimes for hours, sometimes for a couple of days. This caused me an anguish of anxiety. I walked across the *colline*, across the fields, calling. No sign of her, no sound. She came back in the end, just as I'd given up hope. She appeared suddenly, trotting lightly on small white paws, looking unconcerned. She was valiant in her attempts to find a foothold in the house, a place to rest. She was determined to be accepted. She told herself, 'Keep trying. Keep going. It'll all work out in the end.'

She was right. In the end, she was a card-carrying member of the household.

21

After I'd lived in my house for a while, I began to know my neighbours. They were all farmers, *paysans*, middle-aged to elderly. The farms were small plots of land intensively cultivated. Most of the young people had gone away to work in factories or other businesses—or to be unemployed.

My neighbours made me aware of a Provence that had nothing to do with restored old farmhouses and green swimming pools—nor even with painters of Provence, except for Vincent Van Gogh.

This Provence had, years ago, been a land of rocks and stones and thin dry earth threatening to bring the desert north, out of Africa, doing its best to defeat the people who tried to work it. Then, in the sixteenth century, a man of genius, Adam de Crappone, conceived the idea of bringing water to the region in canals. A great network of canals, large and small, dug between the Durance river and the sea, has made every farm fertile. In places, every field is surrounded by a stream.

The water comes from the Durance, into which, in the spring, flow the melting snows from the Alps. It is stored in huge underground caverns so that, in this corner of Provence, there will never be a drought again. Whenever I went on my walks with Caramel I saw the sunlight flashing on strongly flowing streams and I heard the downhill splash of water as it fell from level to level in the hilly country.

In the summer, Mas des Chats echoed with the cool sound of little waterfalls and water running fast through a narrow channel. The melted alpine snows glittered in the heat-stunned garden.

'Before they made the canals,' roared my neighbour, Monsieur Corbet, 'this place was a desert. A desert!'

His extreme deafness made him shout and his voice rose to a crescendo as he bellowed the last words, '*Un désert!*' Visions of the stark Sahara floated before my eyes. I could see red dust burying the orchards and the fertile fields of lettuces and melons and beans and tomatoes and cabbages and aubergines.

Monsieur Corbet and his wife had worked like slaves all their lives,

French beans were the speciality of Monsieur Corbet and his wife. They led the water from the canal furrow by furrow along the rows.

aching backs bent, faces graven with the heat of the sun and the lash of the Mistral. Like all the farmers around me, apart from ploughing with a tractor, they did everything by hand. They planted each seed in its place, hoed, weeded, sprayed, fertilised, led the water from the canal furrow by furrow along the rows and rows of French beans, which were their speciality. Then they picked and carried basket after heavy basket until their cool garage was filled with a great green bounty of vegetables.

Monsieur Corbet would proudly show me his abundant produce, pulling damp cloths off the surface of the baskets, as if he were revealing gold bars. In the afternoon he drove the vegetables down to the little market at the nearby village of St Etienne du Grès. With luck, the entire picking would be sold that evening. Not all farmers were lucky. Sometimes there was a glut of one vegetable or another. All the hard work, the passionate relationship with the earth and the plants were for nothing, that day.

It seemed to me there was more to this relationship than the business of earning a living. The men and women had, I thought, an obsession with the land, giving all of themselves to the handling of earth and the growing of crops. They hated to sell their fields, even those lying waste and empty for lack of labour. They hung on to them as if to members of their family, even if they were offered more than the market price.

They'd always been poor in these parts. The farmers here remembered the hardships of their childhood and fear remained in their hearts. The fear was of failing crops, of plant diseases and insect pests, of debts and penury. Although they were now protected against sickness and old age by the social security system, they could remember the times when the serious illness of one member might have meant financial ruin for the entire family and when old age might bring miserable deprivation.

In this Provence, the farmers were haunted by ghosts of the past. Madame Corbet was the child of a shepherd, her father a poor Italian immigrant. In the spring, the flock of sheep had to be walked from the sun-dried low land to Alpine meadows and brought down again in the autumn as the rains began to fall. She'd walked, each year, with the family and the sheep, a tired child in thin or broken shoes, those endless miles. It wasn't surprising she was frugal and sparing in all her ways, disciplined and hard on herself. The Corbets' cat, Frisquette, came to steal food from my privileged animals, because at home she ate so plainly.

Watching Frisquette eat, I could see the same frugality, the same painful cherishing of choice morsels as I could see in her master and mistress. I was sometimes irritated by Madame Corbet's inability to grasp that times had changed. I wished she could lash out occasionally in an abandon of extravagance. She could afford to—but didn't dare.

Then I felt remorseful. I watched the care she took of her few neat clothes, her restraints, the severe lines on her face, her tired hands. Her greatest pleasures were to gather wild asparagus, wild leeks, mushrooms in their seasons. She would never get over her childhood—nor would any of them, the men and women who worked in the fields near Mas des Chats.

So I became aware of anxiety—an anxiety that drove these people to continue a tradition of physical hardship and passionate labour. Somehow, the anxiety was absorbed by me—undefined, irrational. Anxiety sharpened the sharp edges of the hills, intensified the intense light, the smell of herbs in the *garrigue*, the wind rustling in the canes. I became as sensitive and vulnerable as any of my cats—and it was towards them that I directed my anxiety.

I was anxious about all the cats, but it was Bruno who sometimes caused me a turmoil of agitation. When he was about a year old, towards the end of my second winter in Provence, he became seriously ill. At the start, he lost his appetite and seemed exhausted—so unusual for him, I took him to the vet. Monsieur Lamartin at once noticed how very pale his gums and conjunctivae were and thought perhaps he was suffering from leukaemia. But a blood count showed that the illness was something else—difficult to diagnose. Both red and white cells of his blood were very far below the normal level and it was thought he might have been poisoned. Monsieur Lamartin gave him an injection of antibiotics and cortisone and I took him home. That night he began to vomit. All through the night, at regular intervals, he vomited. Mercifully, after each bout, he drank some water and endured, patiently and courageously, until at last in the morning the vomiting stopped and he slept. We went again to see Monsieur Lamartin in the late afternoon. By then he had a high fever. He was given another injection of antibiotics and cortisone.

Later that night he began to suffer extremely severe abdominal pain. Poor Bruno dragged himself around, crawling on the floor in a desperate attempt to find relief. In the end, after trying and failing to make him comfortable, I picked him up. I lay on my bed and placed him gently on my body. Very gradually, the warmth of my body

93

Unlike most other cats, Bruno accepted the treatment of his illness philosophically. He was trusting and calm.

relaxed the terrible spasms of his gut. I was fully dressed and not very comfortable but I dared not move. At last, he slept. I, too, dozed and woke, dozed and woke. In the morning, he seemed a little better. We went again to the vet, and again and again, each morning for many days. Each day he received an injection of powerful antibiotics and steroids. Slowly a little pink colour returned to his mouth and eyes— a pink which gradually deepened to a normal rose. After two weeks the treatment had to be stopped because he developed ulcers in his skin at the site of the injections. But by then he was better. For a while, he wore a large handkerchief tied round his neck to protect the ulceration of his skin. He rather enjoyed this scarf, sporting it in a jolly way, sailor fashion. The ulcers healed, at last, and he was cured.

Bruno, unlike most other cats, accepted the treatment of his illness philosophically. He was trusting and calm, turning his good, honest face towards me as if he expected me to help him. 'Of course I don't like any of this,' he seemed to say, 'but I understand it's supposed to be curing me.'

During that illness a bond formed between us—a bond which tied me to him for the years to come, and him to me. We became mutually dependent on one another. It was with this dependence that my anxiety was focused on him. I wanted, obsessively, all my cats to be well and thriving. In Bruno, I seemed to feel a particular vulnerability. After his illness, I found his absences, his excursions into the fields and his visits to the neighbours, hard to bear. When he was away—or invisible —for many hours, I worried about him. My anxiety deepened as time went by and there was no sign of him. I'd call, I'd search for him. Sometimes I found him far away, tucked under a bush in the rough vegetation of the *colline*. Sometimes he came if I called. But if he didn't appear and the hours passed, I felt frantic. Then, suddenly, strangely, calm came over me. Not long afterwards, Bruno turned up. In my bondage to him, a mysterious telepathy existed. I knew—or my body knew—when he was near. What blissful relief, what intense pleasure to see him, little brown cat, strolling across the grass or terrace or sliding in at the open window.

'Bruno, where have you been?'

'Out,' he seemed to reply enigmatically, turning a bland and innocent face in my direction.

Why had I become so anxious about him? Was I aware of the special fragility of his charming life?

Did I associate his absences with some fearful anxieties of my childhood? I couldn't say. All I knew was that I was deeply attached to him —and he to me. He made his affection for me clear. But he continued, mercifully, with his independent cat activities. However unhappy I was when he wasn't around, I had to accept that cats are cats and lead their secret lives—although my inclination was to tie him to me with a foolproof chain.

22

Caramel needed no chains. She never left my side if she could possibly
help it. When I drove off in the car, she stationed herself under the
trees near the letter-boxes and waited for me to come back.

Only nightfall and rain made her return to the house. People arriving
on the little road could tell if I were at home by whether Caramel was
sitting under the trees or not.

All ten cats would stretch out, collapsed, without moving, until the sun began to go down in
the late afternoon.

She enjoyed, ecstatically, a brushing of her short-haired, lion-coloured coat—a completely new experience for her. Although her little body was malformed and fragile, she had a brilliant mind. She made every effort to understand what pleased me and what upset me in her behaviour. In the past, she and Violette had rampaged around the neighbourhood, barking hysterically and unreasonably for hours at a time. This was, for her, an exciting and agreeable hobby which she didn't particularly want to give up. But she did give it up at my earnest request.

She asked to be allowed to bark at a few selected visiting cats and dogs. The *chats de la maison*, the ten beautiful cats, she recognised immediately and was entirely indifferent to them. They, in turn, previously very nervous of her, discovered she was harmless.

Baby, who became confused in moments of great excitement—on a walk, for example—sometimes rubbed her little body up against Caramel, much to the dog's embarrassment.

Caramel, squirming slightly, didn't want to be rude to Baby. She could see she meant no harm, but somehow, it wasn't quite right. Anyway, she didn't really like it.

In the summer, the deep walls of the house kept the place cool. Outside, a burning sun shone from a blue sky. Unlike some other Mediterranean areas, there was hardly ever humidity in the air, unless the wind blew from the south, from the sea. No thin vapour of cloud masked the sky or made the distances misty. The landscape was sharp and clear and the sky bright. The cats, all ten, preferred to lie in the shade of bushes in the garden or under the cypresses. They would stretch out, collapsed, without moving, until the sun began to go down in the late afternoon.

Then they would lazily assemble for the evening meal.

23

The cats appeared in the kitchen for breakfast and supper.

In between mealtimes there were some, not all, who demanded or begged for food. Rosie took it for granted she'd be fed at two-hourly intervals during her waking hours. She may have had some abnormality of digestion, she seemed so anxious to eat whenever possible. If she heard me in the kitchen, however late it was, she'd rush headlong from wherever she'd been sleeping to claim that she was fainting, if not dying of low blood sugar.

'No, Rosie. You've had eighteen meals today and not long ago you had some Whiskas *au gibier!*'

Rosie gave a pitiful cry. Did I mean her to go to bed on an empty stomach? Some people were really callous. She happened to know there was an open tin of a pâté which she adored—well, adore was too strong a word, but she did eat it. Yes, yes—OK, it was the last. Yes, she wouldn't ask for another morsel. Yes, she promised. Well then, thank you, at last! . . . and she began, with her usual delicacy, to nibble Kit-e-Kat *au poisson*.

Lily pointed out that the Whiskas I had given her was 'with kidney'. Didn't I know that she never ate 'with kidney'?

'I thought you might this time as it's "made in England". I thought it would remind you of Hampshire. I bought it specially for you. I drove a long way to find it. I was very pleased to see some tins of Whiskas "made in England". I thought it'd be the same for you.'

Lily could hardly believe her ears. But if she didn't like 'with kidney' in Hampshire, why should she like it here? Anyway, she indicated, *I* might have been pleased to see some tins labelled 'made in England'; she wasn't so sure about herself.

'Very well. Forget it. Here's one *"au lapin"*.'

Lily seemed to think that was better—well, a little. What she really liked was prawns—prawns and cream.

'You can't live on prawns and cream. Better eat the *lapin*.'

She was eating it, wasn't she? That wasn't to say she liked it.

'Very well. But just eat it, there's a good girl and have done. I can't

What Lily really liked was prawns—prawns and cream.

go on opening tins all night—and anyway, it's too expensive.'

She let me know it wasn't her fault that I liked the look of tins 'made in England—with kidney'. She had made it crystal clear she didn't care for 'with kidney'.

'No. Yes. Well, perhaps the French cats would like it. Yes, thank heavens they do.'

Lily pointed out that there was no accounting for tastes. She only knew what she liked—and she thought I'd find that Rosie agreed with her. There! Did I see?

The girl in the shop was right.

'*Les chats sont difficiles,*' she said.

Rosie claimed, with dignity, that she was not *difficile*. All I had to do was give her well cooked *merlu blanc* or *colin lieu* over and over again, a few grams at a time—bought at a decent shop, of course—alternating with *au lapin* or perhaps *au thon*, or those sardines *en gelée* from Thailand and a little *crème longue durée* with warm water—the milk being so horrible here, why was it?—and then *merlu blanc* again. She didn't consider herself in the least difficult although, of course, her standards were high.

And by the way, why was it I never gave them that delicious fresh coley, beautifully cooked, which Nancy used to serve them back home?

'And you say you're not difficult! I'm sorry that Nancy ever served you coley. As I'm always telling you, it ruined your eating habits.'

At this Rosie's pathetic expression reminded me that she'd had problems with food from an early age and that I'd forgotten that very special diet her English doctor had ordered for her—hard-boiled eggs, sponge cake, cheese, boiled rice with a little butter, never to touch tinned food—and that Monsieur Lamartin here had recommended *crème glacée* in her hearing.

'These veterinarians have their fanciful ideas. I wonder what they give their own cats?'

Rosie primly insisted that she was a special case, an invalid with a very delicate digestion.

'*You*—an invalid?'

To prove her point, Rosie began to retch and vomit. The recently ingested *thon en gelée*, including a sprig of dried grass and a little matted hair, was deposited on a newly cleaned rug at the foot of the staircase.

Having got rid of the tinned cat food, she at once made it plain that a little *merlu blanc* wouldn't come amiss. She needed something to calm her stomach.

She watched me until I'd meekly placed a saucer of fish in front of her. Then she began to nibble delicately, one morsel at a time.

Bruno was always impatient—or even passionate—about his food, as he was passionate in all his dealings with the world. But, as always, he was cheerful about it.

Now he was under the impression he'd heard someone say something about tea time. A little fish for him, please, or cheese ought to do—or a little of each, perhaps?

'No, Bruno. It's not tea time. You'll have to wait.'

He turned an innocent face towards me, making out that his hearing was getting very poor, he couldn't think why.

He leapt on to the kitchen counter by the sink as he always did. One skilful bound and he was in position.

Had I said I was finding him a little fish? He was really peckish. Most grateful, he was.

He crooned a little to himself while waiting and gazed out of the back window.

He was completely confident that he'd be fed. He was right. His bonhomie, his charm, made him irresistible.

He discovered he could manage to make the roll of kitchen paper, attached to a holder, spin round and round.

When he wanted to draw attention to himself, he sat on his hind legs and, with his front paws, sent the roll flying wildly round and round—until, full of laughter, I attended to his needs. Because I laughed and because he understood he amused me, he happily repeated his turn. The kitchen roll spun vigorously. He was like someone rapping the table in a restaurant to call the waiter.

'Waiter!' Bruno spun the roll briskly.

He succeeded in getting attention because, although he didn't unfurl the roll, his sharp claws made ribbons of the paper.

Several of the cats were particularly fussy about their likes and dislikes.

Baby liked half-cooked fish, warm and soft.

Maman slurped up a mixture of mince, liver and fish with some difficulty, after most of her rotting teeth had been drawn. She wouldn't touch tinned catfood.

Only Oedipus would gulp down almost anything and everything, crying with hunger before he was fed. His cry reminded me of newly born lambs in a field with their mothers.

'Maaa,' called Oedipus, trying to climb up my legs with the urgency of his need for food. 'Maaa,' he bleated again and again. If he sounded very distressed, Hélène would run to him and begin licking his head

101

Several of the cats were particularly fussy about their food. Only Oedipus would gulp down almost anything and everything.

gently, and his ears. He received her tender attention gratefully—but quickly returned to his crying and demanding. If all the cats were hungry, there was pandemonium. The anxiety of one to be fed was transferred to another. All wanted food simultaneously. Even Maman joined the throng. She told Baby there was no use letting themselves be pushed aside. They had to stand up for themselves or they'd be the last to eat. Besides, there was such a thing as self-respect . . .

Misti cat, Topcat, Pumky and Griffy, Ron Ron, Caress, Filou and Divin, Griffiz, Pickit, Fido, Friskies, Lycat, Cat Régal, Freddy, Loyal, Sweety, Birman—these were only some of the names in the great proliferation of tinned cat foods which took place a year or two after I came to Provence. When I first arrived I was glad to see basic and familiar brands—Whiskas, Kit-e-Kat, Friskies and Sheba. Not much else was available. There were modest arrangements of pet foods in the supermarkets and people bought them on a small scale.

Then suddenly, it seemed, the French nation took to giving their pets tinned food.

That was the signal for an avalanche of new products to arrive in the markets. Animal food shelves extended and extended and occupied whole sections of the floor space.

Like everyone else, I tried out many of the new varieties on my ten cats at Mas des Chats.

Most of them were turned down out of hand—hardly sniffed at before rejected—how conservative are cats and yet insatiable for variety.

But some of the new brands of cat food found favour with at least a few of the cats and one or two were enthusiastically accepted by all.

The hardest to please was Baby. She had a habit of asking for food at ten-minute intervals, crying and squeaking and imploring as if she were starving. Then she was likely to turn away at once from the dish I offered her—or, if she did accept it, she'd eat a morsel or two and then go away. Sometimes she rejected everything and pitifully turned her attention to a dish of dry biscuits. They knew how to blackmail me, my beautiful cats!

I was an easy victim and they never abandoned their efforts to persuade me to try something else, open yet another tin, please, the last one was inedible, probably bad, poisoned wouldn't be surprised, but anyway, horrible.

24

While I tried to understand and enter the thoughts and dreams of my beautiful cats they, in turn, did their best to understand me. Caramel, too, studied me and my behaviour with scrupulous care.

There were certain of my activities which they found completely baffling, although they tried to make sense of them.

Firstly, there was the way I kept changing my clothes. They were always having to wait for attention while I took off jackets or dressing-gowns or shoes, substituting garments which seemed to them no different from the first.

Then there was the telephone. They were very puzzled by the fact that, at a certain signal, I rushed to the instrument and began talking, sometimes at length, to myself.

They discussed this quietly with one another.

The ringing or fluting of the telephone alarmed them and they were irritated and impatient if I went into a long conversation (a monologue as they saw it) just as they were expecting a meal.

Then, one day, Nero, with a gleam in his golden eyes, found a solution to this problem. The telephone in the kitchen stood on a large tiled table. Nero discovered that if he sidled around long enough, purring like a lion, rubbing himself against me and the telephone while I was having a conversation with someone, and if he made large tramping movements with his great paws, he might accidentally on purpose lean on or stamp on the button which broke the connection. In mid-sentence, I was cut off. Nero was very pleased and the other cats, gathered round and waiting for their meal, applauded him.

Even Rosie, who deliberately snubbed Nero most of the time, remembering his old bad habits, felt temporarily warmly disposed to him, then pointedly suggested to me we might now get on with the suppers.

Dear Rosie! One of her most endearing characteristics was that she hated rows among the humans. She herself had many a tiff and squabble with the other cats of the household, but she couldn't bear human discord. If she heard voices raised in anger she ran from one to the other of those disputing, crying and squeaking in her high-pitched little voice.

She was so distressed that she usually succeeded in putting an end to the row amid laughter—but then she needed to be comforted and reassured.

Not that there were many rows. I was alone most of the time, acting, as far as they were concerned, simply as their very loved and devoted servant.

Maman was accustomed to being brushed and groomed each evening. She used to try to persuade me to attend to her just at the very moment I was busy doing the washing up of all their dirty dishes and mine. She came into the kitchen again and again, and when I wouldn't drop everything and go to brush her, she showed her irritation by clawing at a rug. She couldn't imagine, she complained to Baby, what Dr Reinhold was doing each evening, splashing about in that water hole, wearing those silly pink gloves and marching endlessly —and pointlessly—up and down beside their food counter.

Only Bruno, I think, knew me—and tried to know me better—in my own right.

And Caramel, of course, who felt bound to respect me as an authority.

High in the sky above the Alpilles, wings spread flat on the crystal air, a buzzard cruised, his bright eyes searching. I watched him dive like a falling stone, then soar again, beak empty. Some small life was spared, only temporarily, perhaps.

I sat on a rock on the highest point of the silent hills above Les Baux.

Down in the valley, the sun glinted on tourist cars. Charabancs let loose their troupes of weary travellers, determined to master the history and geography of the village perched on the summit above them. Out they poured, then trickled into the village which waited greedily for their francs.

At the end of the land the sea shimmered, twenty-five miles away, the chimneys of the oil refinery clearly silhouetted. Where I sat I could turn and look towards the north and see, set in the purple shadows of the plain, the white stones of the Popes' Palace shining in the sun and the course of the Rhône as the river slid sideways into the hills, before making for the sea. A marvellous place, a marvellous view, five minutes by car from the Mas des Chats. Caramel and I congratulated ourselves on our good luck, having all this on our doorstep. Nothing, we agreed, could be more pleasant than the quiet hilltop on a brilliant day, watching the buzzards above and the tourists below, breathing in the high air and the scent of the herbs of the *garrigue*.

25

The local farmers fed their animals inadequately—perhaps as a result of their tradition of poverty, perhaps for vague and confused religious reasons going back to the middle ages. Dogs were often given crusts of dry bread and water as a large part of their daily diet, many cats were hardly fed at all. Cats were supposed to hunt for their food, catching mice and birds. Whatever the reasons, there were many very hungry animals who roamed the countryside round Mas des Chats, searching for food. The bowls I put out at night were polished clean by morning.

Other people also fed starving animals. Every now and then I fell into conversation with shoppers in the cat and dog food section of the local supermarkets. In this way, I met one woman who had fifteen cats, another seventeen. Most of the foreigners in the neighbourhood, whom I gradually came to know, had adopted strays—lost or abandoned cats and dogs.

I might have predicted what was to happen at Mas des Chats. When I was searching for a suitable house, a local agent took me to see an isolated farmhouse in wild country, far from any village or town.

The house was empty, echoing, sad. The owner, a lonely old farmer, widowed long ago, had died a few weeks before my visit. His only son lived far away. The son had come, with his wife, to bury the old man and to take away furniture and farm machinery. The house was put up for sale.

The son and his wife were at the house when I and the agent arrived. They were on the point of returning to their own home. A few last possessions were being loaded into a waiting van.

They were ready to go. They shook hands, warmly. They climbed into the van. The engine revved. They shouted goodbye.

That was the moment when I saw the cat. Elderly, small and humble, a little grey cat, the old man's cat, stood forlornly in the open doorway of the empty house. 'Your cat,' I shouted. 'You've forgotten your cat!'

The young man leaned from the window of the van and laughed

kindly. 'No, no,' he said. 'We can't take *her* . . . We can't possibly take her . . .'

'But what will become of her? You can't leave her like this! She'll starve to death . . .'

He laughed again.

'She'll go to the neighbours,' he said. 'She knows her way around' . . . and they drove away.

I turned to the house agent.

'I know,' he said uncomfortably. 'People do that sometimes here . . . or anywhere . . . I myself have come to bring her food and water when there was no one here. Even on Sunday, I came . . .'

Silence fell between us, a silence intensified by the silent land around us and the silence of the hills. We looked at the cat. The cat looked at us. Her look poignantly conveyed the helpless plight, the sadness and the reproach of every animal on earth betrayed by man.

Then, suddenly fearful, she ran off and was gone.

There were many like her, of course—cats and dogs who'd once had caring owners and who were then abandoned for one reason or another. They became wild, or half wild, although they kept in themselves the elements of their former relationships with men and women. They could quite easily be made tame again—almost. My beautiful cats remained wary, ready for flight, prepared for hurt. They lent themselves temporarily to trust and love, but they remembered their injuries.

26

Under Bruno's leadership the ten cats slowly settled into a close community. Each had his or her place in the hierarchy, each related to the others—except for Katy, forever an outcast. But Katy did join us when we took a walk in the vineyard. She was an enthusiastic walker and dashed out of the undergrowth as soon as she saw the convoy assemble.

I usually took this walk with the cats in the late afternoon, towards sunset.

At Ashford Rosie would spend hours in the undergrowth, invisible, immune to my cries and appeals that she come home.

In the old days, at Ashford, Rosie and Lily and Mews and I also took walks. We'd go round the cornfield at the back of the house and up to the woods, single file like Indians. Sometimes we walked along the line of the trees, but I was nervous of leading them deep into the woods. Lily liked to take this walk on her own, occasionally. From the house I could see her little white shape, brilliant against the dark of the trees, as she strolled along the bank or sat, fixed as a statue, beside a mouse or rabbit hole.

The cats loved the walks in England and were delighted, in France, to be taken around the vineyard. Rosie would suggest, if she felt so inclined, that a little exercise was healthy.

A walk, she seemed to say, would be in order now. Fresh air would do them all good.

I reminded her that she'd been out all night—'You were in the fields when I went to bed and I had to fetch you from farmer Savin's melon plantation at breakfast time!'

She in turn reminded me that she'd had a refreshing sleep since then.

Rosie very much enjoyed hunting at Ashford. She'd spend hours under the beech hedge, hours in the undergrowth invisible, immune to my cries and appeals that she come home.

In France, she disappeared into the nearby fields again, pretending to be deaf to my calls—giving a bad example to the younger cats, as I told her. This criticism she brushed aside. She was only acting according to her instincts, she implied. 'But Baby, who adores and imitates you, would make a splendid cat under your guidance. All she needs is a little licking into shape . . .'

This didn't stop Rosie from giving Baby a sharp tap with her paw as she passed innocently by.

'Oh, Rosie,' I sighed, 'a touch of tolerance!'

Rosie shrugged me off, demanding to know whether we were going on a walk or not.

We all set off, the ten beautiful cats walking softly and deftly through what must have seemed to them like a jungle of the Amazon. Tall grass, wild plants of the fields, long tendrils of vine made a thick tangle of undergrowth. Neatly they stepped, their bodies perfectly orientated, limbs in line, never the slightest error in their judgement of space and objects.

Sometimes they'd collapse into a patch of dry and crumbling earth, rolling ecstatically. Sometimes they'd sit for a while meditating, tails curled tightly around their feet. Then on at a run, at a gallop, bright and keen. Some walked in Indian file, some took their own paths. Katy opted for cover, hurrying from one shelter to the next, nervous of being attacked by Monsieur le Gris. Monsieur le Gris was a bully. Bullied himself and harassed by Bruno, he took his disgruntlement out on the younger cats. Katy was his chosen victim. He was four times her size and ten times her weight. I don't think Monsieur le Gris ever recognised he was a Centurion tank of a cat. Emotionally, he was so childlike and so insecure, he didn't realise how formidable he actually was. He'd throw himself on Katy, if he got the chance, once hurting her badly. She was terrified of him but, brave as a lion, she didn't give up. She'd spit and snarl furiously when he tried to attack her, screaming French obscenities which she must have picked up as an infant in the gutter. On the walks, she tried to keep out of his way, sheltering behind the vines. I protected her.

Bruno was the leader. He marched at the head of the column. Every now and then he created diversions. He might bury himself impetuously in a deep clump of grass. Then he'd leap out unexpectedly as another member of the group walked innocently past.

Rosie rebuked Bruno sharply, fussily restoring her startled hair to its proper place. But she really rather liked the excitement. Lily, always ready to have the vapours at a whisper or the drop of a pin, rushed off at a tangent, squeaking. Baby, who adored Bruno and his madcap escapades, tried to turn the whole thing into a game of catchers.

Nero, after giving a dignified start, strode on, his head in the air.

Monsieur le Gris was offended and grumbled. Katy was too busy taking care of herself to notice.

Maman, stomping forward determinedly, called to Baby to remember her manners, dear—and drew back her skirts as she passed the bubbling Bruno. Hélène and Oedipus kept to the outskirts of the group and so missed the fun.

111

When Bruno leapt out at him unexpectedly, Monsieur le Gris was offended and grumbled.

The setting sun often arranged an especially dramatic scene as a background to the walk. The whole sky was diffused with lilac, while gold, rose and green stained the western horizon. All was incandescent in the clear and brilliant light of Provence. Apricot and primrose, vermilion and scarlet took over when the sun had gone and, pure as fire, flared and flamed and slowly died. Against the sky, the black cypresses stood, like citadels, like cathedrals.

The cats, unaware of this glory, had thoughts of home and supper. Bruno suddenly reared up like a serpent from his nest in the grass, blue squinting eyes rolling wildly, then flew like a deer or a race horse towards the house, the beautiful cats following at their own pace. All finally assembled in the kitchen for the evening meal.

27

Before the dawn and at intervals all day long we could hear, at Mas des Chats, cocks crowing, calling from farm to farm at the foot of the Alpilles. For me their cry was poignant, reminding me of my South African childhood. I remembered the sound as belonging to remote farms, with an isolated homestead set in a great tract of lonely land. The sound of the cocks crowing was linked in my mind to other sounds of human habitation in a wilderness. There was the clunk of a wind-driven water pump at a borehole, the metal blades turning idly in the breeze—and the same intermittent breeze rustling the leaves of a few tall eucalyptus trees. There was also the drowsy buzz of flies at the screened door of the farmhouse kitchen in the heat of a summer afternoon.

The cockerels paused and rested. The wind dropped. The sounds of the pump and the lifted eucalyptus leaves fell into an immense silence. That silence and the extreme remoteness, the many empty miles of grass or bush or scrub or desert, drew me compellingly to return. Would I ever return? I thought not.

So, in Provence, I heard with some sadness the cocks crowing in the calm but populated silence of Mas des Chats. The hens roamed free on many of the farms, which was, I suppose, why the *communes* regularly put out poisons for the foxes and other predators.

Occasionally, driving home late over the Alpilles, I'd see a fox in the beam of the headlights. From time to time, in winter, we heard one bark. Caramel went mad, barking wildly in return.

At night, owls hooted in Provence. Once, when I was giving Jasmin his morning bowl of bread and carrots, a large owl flew up out of the tree above our heads, pale, fluffy and alarmed.

I and the cats were also alarmed for a moment—then I, at least, was happy to see it.

28

Bruno had a range of fluting cries by means of which he let me know his feelings and needs and views.

'Hello! Very pleased to see you. Thought you were never coming back.'

'I say, I'm famished! What about lunch?'

'A bit of a cuddle would be nice, don't you think?'

'Any chance of us taking a walk?' and, after his serious illness, 'I'm exhausted. I'd be truly grateful if you could give me a lift.'

I grew to understand his conversation and I responded in a way that seemed to satisfy him.

He was so gentle, I thought of him as a Candide of the cat tribe, believing all was for the best in the best of all possible worlds.

He—and all the other beautiful cats—had the innocence of wild creatures; and they were, of course, half wild—to the frustration of the vet, Monsieur Lamartin, when he came to treat or vaccinate them, and with the exception of Rosie!

I was enchanted to see the cats making concessions to human beings as they did when they were affectionate or teasing or played with the toys I gave them.

Bruno moved easily from jungle to garden. Nothing was more warming than his intense welcome when I arrived home after an absence. His purr went from soft rumble to deep bass hum.

'Thrilled to see you! Missed you very much.'

He too went on his outings. My welcome home was different from his. 'Bruno! Where *have* you been? You've been away for hours. Why do you make me so anxious?'

He'd look at me with his pure and steady blue-eyed gaze.

I had my world, he always seemed to say, and he had his. There were areas where we would not meet. He had things to do, thoughts to think which I couldn't understand. It was the same for me. I should accept it, leave it at that and give him some credit for being able to manage on his own without my help. He knew his way around there. After all, he'd been there for a few years now and he'd learned a

Bruno moved easily from jungle to garden, from wildness to affectionate domesticity.

thing or two about the neighbourhood. That wasn't to say he didn't appreciate my concern—but he thought I overdid it . . .

He was right. I was too anxious, too afraid of losing this silky little cat.

29

When I first moved to Provence I'd hoped to find a person, or perhaps man and wife, who'd help me look after the place, look after the cats and stand in for me when I wanted to travel. These people were not intended to replace the gardener or the *femme de ménage*, whom I greatly valued. Their duties were mainly concerned with the animals. There was a little two-roomed house in the garden—a charming house, with a pleasant, peaceful atmosphere. Here, I hoped to lodge the helpers. I can't remember exactly whom I had in mind, the dream person or people I might employ, because the reality later obscured the dream.

It proved to be almost impossible to find responsible and reliable helpers. People came and went, living for a while in the little house. Once established there, they weren't prepared to give me any service in return for lodging. The people I chose, or who chose me, turned out to be disturbed, sad, misfits, drifters, on the edge of society.

The first was a young man called Antonio. Spanish, sombre and unstable, he was sent to me by a friend who worked in an estate agency, where he'd gone to look for lodgings. She telephoned to say, 'There's a young man here who's really looking for something to rent which is difficult to find at the moment. I've explained your position. He seems willing to try to help you in return for your little house. He's pleasant. I think he runs a business of some sort in one of the market towns not far away. He's a businessman, he says. May I send him round? He's very good-looking, by the way! He says he likes cats! And he's born in France although his parents were Spanish . . .'

Antonio arrived. A tall, elegant figure emerged with dignity from an immensely dilapidated old Renault car. A dark, tragic young man, hesitant and insecure, but with a regal manner, he inspected the little house.

I explained about the help I needed. His 'business' in the town turned out to be a café owned by his elder sister, where Antonio was her right-hand man. He served coffees, swept the floor, took the money to the bank, chatted to the customers. He could easily attend to the cats in the mornings, but in the evenings the café was busy. In times of emergency, however, he could quickly drive over, feed the cats and return to his duties. In exchange for the help he'd give me, he'd live in comfort in the well furnished little house, rent free. Nothing was put in writing: it was a verbal agreement between gentlemen.

How ignorant, how absurd I was! The cats were immediately up in arms.

Baby made it clear to me that they all felt they didn't need him. She raced away at the sight of him. Rosie was even more vehement. Was I really thinking of handing them over to him? She gathered he was a Spaniard! Hadn't I heard about bull-fighting? The cruellest nation on earth!

Bruno let me know gently that they didn't need anyone else, they were very, very satisfied with what I did for them.

Lily had an attack of the vapours as soon as he appeared and then vanished under the nearest bed.

Only Maman sensibly accepted that food was food, and Nero agreed with her.

The other cats had not, as yet, joined the household.

At the start I was present at the cat-feeding sessions, showing Antonio who ate what. The cats, in a united gesture of no confidence, didn't turn up for breakfast until Antonio had left for work.

In the beginning Antonio was pleasant, skilful and co-operative. We prepared plates of food for the cats which they'd eat as soon as he went off to the town. I can still see him standing gamely at the kitchen counter snipping up bits of liver with a pair of scissors, elegantly opening tins of cat food.

We talked as we stood there. He told me the story of his life. His father was a Spanish builder who had brought his wife and family to France in the hopes of finding work. Antonio, the youngest child, was born after they'd crossed the border. When he was two years old, his mother died suddenly. His father immediately went back to Spain, leaving the French state to take care of his five children. Antonio was separated from his brothers and sisters and put in a foster home with other orphans. There he remained for four years.

'Were they kind to you?'

'Oh—so-so—strict—I don't really remember . . .'

When he was six years old, an organisation set up to unite the children of broken families found him and took him to live with his brothers and sisters, some much older than he was. One sister was particularly kind and loving and acted as a mother to him. It was this sister who owned the café where he now worked. Hearing this story, I understood the darkness that shadowed Antonio's life and the pain that showed in his vulnerable face. I think he worked quite hard at the café which was near the station in the town. He told me it was mostly schoolchildren who came there for coffee and cold drinks and ice cream. But in the basement his sister ran an illegal poker game. It was this that brought in the money.

Not long after Antonio was established in the little house, a small, jaunty car was to be seen parked outside it in the evenings and at week-ends. The car belonged to a young, smiling blonde girl. Before she appeared Antonio had been helpful and pleasant. He had continued to prepare the cats' morning food with me (in the absence of the cats) and they ate when he'd left for the café. Sometimes, he telephoned me from the café. Was I all right? Did I need anything? Should he bring me a loaf of bread? It was he who taught me that the largest shape of a long white loaf was called a *restaurant*. But after the arrival of the blonde girl and the jaunty little car I saw very little of Antonio. When I did see him he was surly, grumpy and childish. Instead of looking clean and cared for as he normally did (I remember how carefully he had ironed his shirts), he was red-eyed and dishevelled.

It was winter. The little house was always shut, the windows firmly closed. He and the girl seemed locked in, condensation trickling down the overheated window panes.

Antonio gave up helping me with the morning cat dishes. The cats rejoiced. They appeared smartly on time the moment I came down into the kitchen.

One Sunday, at midday, Antonio's sister telephoned from the café and asked to speak to him. I went to fetch him.

The girl's car was parked on the gravel beside his elderly Renault. The house was shut and silent. I spent some time knocking on the shutters trying to rouse him. He appeared at last, belatedly pulling on a small pair of white see-through underpants. He was otherwise naked. He looked bewildered, confused, shaken out of some deep sleep, staring at me with eyes that hardly recognised me. The mention of his sister seemed to galvanise him and he went to fetch slippers and a dressing-gown. I returned to the telephone to tell his sister he was on his way. I also said I'd like to see her when convenient for her.

She came to visit me one evening while Antonio worked at the café. She was a pleasant looking, pleasant mannered, tidy and respectable young woman. We talked about Antonio. 'I'm afraid,' I said, 'he may be taking drugs.'

She looked at once dismayed, upset. Had Antonio had any visitors? she asked. A young blonde girl in a little Citroën, new, metallic bronze?

Then yes, she said, such a thing was not impossible. It had happened before, with this same girl. It was she who was responsible for his wildness. There had been a crisis. His sister had told Antonio he must give up the café or give up the girl. He had given up the girl and turned over a new leaf.

'What kind of girl is this?' I asked. 'What kind of parents to let this very young person stay out all night, all weekend, without seeming to notice or care?'

Well-to-do parents, said Antonio's sister, who gave their daughter money but didn't bother to find out what she was doing with it, didn't care what happened to her. Her mother suffered from depression and left her daughter to go her own way . . .

I said I was sorry but Antonio must leave my little house. She agreed. It seemed that in any case he must leave shortly. He'd bought —or she'd bought for him—an apartment in a block that was being built in the town. This was almost ready. Meanwhile, she would house him or make some other arrangement for him.

There was a pause.

She looked at me strangely.

Might she ask me a question?

'Of course.'

Had I spent New Year's Eve with Antonio at the Palace Hotel in Cannes and had I given him a diamond watch?

The question was unexpected.

'No,' I said, 'of course not. Antonio spent it with the girl in the little house here.'

She was not quite sure whether to believe me. She still searched me with doubting eyes.

I liked her very much at our meeting. I said, 'Antonio talks rather freely about the poker game in your restaurant. Perhaps he should be more discreet?'

She said it didn't bother her. Everyone who had a café or restaurant in the town ran a poker game. She was up to date with her payments to the little man who she believed paid the police, so she'd nothing to worry about. She paid what she was asked. It was no problem.

Before he left, I talked to Antonio. I told him I'd seen his sister. I told him I knew about his past. I said his sister loved him like a mother and he was a fool to destroy himself. He wept, childlike tears running down his sad face. He said he wanted to give up the girl and reform himself. He'd done this before, successfully. He would go back to his fiancée in the town, and he wouldn't see the blonde girl again.

The outcome was, I believe, good as far as Antonio and his fiancée and sister were concerned. But the blonde girl was unhappy. She telephoned once, talking in a quiet, sad little voice, a child, like Antonio. She asked me if I knew why Antonio had given her up.

I said I couldn't help her but I thought she should respect his decision. If ever she needed help, why not see her doctor and ask to be sent to a psychiatrist?

I felt very sorry for her.

———————◇———————

That was Antonio.

Then there was Denis, who I thought was in love with his sister who had a very young baby, whose mother had died when he was six years old and whose father was an alcoholic engineer. There were the terrible twins, two hopelessly inadequate girls whose mother had been ill when they were infants. The children of the family had all been separated and farmed out to relations or friends for the next three years.

There was Arlette, whose father was a soldier who'd been away from home for seven years without a break while she was a child and whose mother disliked her. The stories of their lives read like pages from a psychiatrist's notebook or a novel of Balzac.

'What next?' cried the cats after each new disastrous arrangement. 'Will you never learn?' But the worst, although not the last, the most dangerous of all, was the railwayman, the *cheminot*.

A French friend said to me, 'Madame Boulanger has an excellent man and wife who look after her. He's a retired railwayman. They say people who worked on the railways all their lives are responsible, very reliable . . .'

I put an advertisement in the journal of the SNCF, the railwaymen's journal. There were several replies. Of these, I chose three possible candidates, who were prepared to come to see me for a preliminary interview. One turned out not to be a railwayman but a professional security guard who worked mainly at night, in Paris. He lived there in a quarter which had been almost taken over by Algerians and Moroccans. He and his wife were two of the few French people who'd remained in the district. He found living there almost unbearable. His wife didn't want to move or leave Paris. They had grown-up children and grandchildren in Paris of whom she was very fond. But he thought that if he found a job and a house and settled somewhere she'd probably join him later. He'd never lived in the country in his life. He only knew city pavements, city squares.

He had a small dog he must bring with him. He loved it dearly. He liked cats also. They had a cat or two. I showed him the little house and while we sat there, talking, Bruno came in and quite took to the sad little man. He was very short, with a thick red beard. Bruno climbed on his knee—unusual for Bruno, but then he was very sensitive to unhappiness and liked to comfort if he could.

I gave this man lunch at a café in the town. The food turned out to be terrible. We could hardly eat it. I had to apologise for it. He drank a little wine, but only a glass or two.

I asked him how he came to read the railwaymen's journal. He said he read everything there was and answered every likely advertisement. He was desperate to get out of his *quartier*. In the late afternoon I took him back to the station at Avignon. He'd taken a day return ticket on the TGV, very expensive. Later I sent him a cheque for the fare.

He stood in the entrance to the station waving to me as I drove away—a little man in his too big tidy raincoat, big thick shoes, shiny with black polish, enormous gloves. I'd said I'd let him know and he was hopeful.

The next candidate turned out to have been a senior executive, an office man in railway administration, just retired. He arrived by the TGV at Avignon, having made a swift journey from a city in the north. A thin, fastidious pleasant man in a narrow brown suit, he seemed modest and cheerful. His story was that he'd left his wife and adolescent children for another woman. This woman was divorced, but she too lived with adolescent children. Monsieur Mathieu had to give his wife and children financial support. He supported also his love, and he had also, of course, to support himself. He lived alone in a rented apartment. In spite of having a good pension, he was short of money.

He had been born in the south, he told me, a farmer's son in the Alpes de Provence. He thought he might like to have a farm himself one day. Meanwhile, when he read my advertisement he'd answered as an attempt at beginning a new life. He was very disciplined, didn't drink or smoke, exercised a great deal, rode a bicycle. He looked younger than his years. We had lunch, this time at a nearby country restaurant. The food was better than the lunch I'd given the nightwatchman. Monsieur Mathieu drank Perrier water, delicately, and ate sparingly but with enjoyment.

Another sad man, he told me his father had resented having a clever, bookish son and was brutal to him. He was rescued by his school teachers. When he left school he went to university, did well and was then accepted in the railway administration. But he'd always longed to return to Provence. He liked the little house and thought there might be possibilities for him at Mas des Chats. He'd take over the maintenance of the vineyard, for instance, which the postman now looked after in return for the grapes.

Bruno took one look at him and decided he wasn't a cat man. I agreed with Bruno—but he was a pleasant, intelligent, interesting

123

The postman looked after my vineyard in return for the grapes.

person. He too waved goodbye from the entrance to Avignon station, an elegant, graceful wave—before taking his seat in a first class compartment on the TGV.

30

The third applicant was called Kupfer, Roland Kupfer. He came originally from Alsace, he told me, but his family had moved to Algeria when he was a small boy and there he'd grown up. He was brought to see me by his nephew with whom he was staying and who lived in Nîmes with his girlfriend and their child. He seemed a cheerful, ordinary man, well preserved for his age, who'd been a goods train driver for many years, on the French railways, now retired. He wore thin-rimmed glasses and a small moustache. He had, I noticed, neat, small hands and feet. He'd brought with him, to show me, some medals which he said he'd received when fighting with the Free French forces in the 1939–1945 War. He'd been a marine, he said. He'd had a hard, poverty-stricken childhood. His father, a railway worker in Algeria, had been injured at work and spent years in hospital with chronic infections of his bones before the days of antibiotics. The Railways had paid only a minimum wage to the family during this time.

Monsieur Kupfer liked the little house. I explained what his duties would be in exchange for the lodging. He was to be a *gardien*, a sort of caretaker. In addition, he was to feed the animals and water the pots of plants on the terrace and do any other little jobs that needed to be done, and a little gardening. For this he'd be paid. Mr Kupfer said he accepted, if I accepted him.

I asked to see him again before deciding. Of the three candidates, I thought him the most suitable.

This time he was brought over from Nîmes by an extremely stout boy, the 'brother-in-law' of his nephew.

Between his two visits he had telephoned. He'd forgotten to tell me, he said, that after retirement he'd worked for three years as the *maître d'hôtel* in a three star hotel in Le Touquet. He could therefore wait at table, help prepare food and be useful generally when I entertained guests. Very encouraging, I thought.

On his second visit Monsieur Kupfer wore a sky-blue track suit, very close fitting, clean and dapper and highly unsuitable for a man of his age and slight portliness. He told me he'd been a keen and efficient footballer in his youth and that now he enjoyed training children. If he got the job, he'd enrol at the local sportsground to teach the game to the schoolboys once a week.

He told me he had a house in Normandy, that he was separated from his wife who lived in a flat by the sea and that he had no children. He liked cats, he said. He'd always kept a cat but, one after another, the local *chasseurs* had destroyed them.

I agreed to take him on—on a trial basis for three months. He would live in the little house as *gardien* without payment. But if he fed the cats, Jasmin and the dogs and did a little light work in the garden he'd be paid, and in either case insured against illness and injury.

The agreement was verbal. Nothing was put in writing, nothing signed. I thought he seemed honest and decent—my great mistake.

We shook hands—and then, on the way to the car, he suddenly said, amiably, 'And must I bring my own olive oil and vinegar?' I was stunned. He's demented, I thought, in disbelieving horror.

I said, 'Monsieur Kupfer, you have to feed yourself. You must provide your own food, olive oil, vinegar, everything!'

He seemed slightly embarrassed, glossed things over, murmured, 'Yes, yes, I understand.'

The fat boy approached. We all shook hands and Monsieur Kupfer was driven away. Oh lord! I thought, have I taken on a brain-damaged old lunatic?

I should, of course, have called the whole thing off immediately. Some weird, unconscious self-destructive urge caused me to persevere. I telephoned the nephew's home. His girlfriend answered.

I said, 'I'm afraid Monsieur Kupfer is mentally unwell. I can't take him on if he's ill.'

At once there was an indignant outburst. 'I assure you, Madame, he is perfectly well. How can you have such an idea? He is perfectly normal. No, his brain is perfectly normal!'

This could not have been so. It later transpired that Monsieur Kupfer had had three attacks of blocking of the arteries of his brain —three small attacks but, nevertheless, they had left him confused, deranged, disturbed. Not unnaturally, the nephew found him difficult to live with, and I did not know that Monsieur Kupfer was standing beside the woman as she spoke to me.

I thought, Well, it's only for three months. Any retired person is likely to have something wrong with him.

I considered the other applicants. The little night watchman from Paris wouldn't know how to occupy himself. He'd be lonely and sad. He had no experience at all of country life. The senior executive would be equally at a loss at Mas des Chats, equally lonely and bored. Those two men dreamed, unrealistically, about life in Provence.

I would give Monsieur Kupfer a try. Very quickly, I could see I'd made a mistake—a mistake which developed into a serious and long drawn-out struggle.

He was, of course, quite unable to do what I needed.

At once he wanted to keep chickens, he wanted to keep rabbits, he wanted a cat. More than all that, he wanted a woman, a kind of housekeeper, slave, companion, perhaps lover.

My kind neighbours, Monsieur and Madame Corbet, were able to persuade him this was no place for chickens. More than the trouble they were worth; they tended to get ill and die; one egg, by the time it was laid, was worth a fortune in terms of labour and chicken feed. Cheaper and easier to buy eggs and chickens at the supermarket.

'No rabbits!' I said firmly.

As regards the cat, he arrived at a time when the other cats were chasing and hunting Katy. I thought it might be a good idea if she had a refuge in the little house. He could care for her as long as he remained there. I would keep an eye on them.

Bruno had inspected Monsieur Kupfer. He was undecided about him. In his good-natured way he was prepared to accept Kupfer's good points, but was, all the same, a little nervous of him. Rosie simply turned her back and refused to go near him, looking at me pityingly when I suggested that Kupfer possibly liked cats. Nero made a little effort to be affectionate—as if they both had known hard times and so, brothers in misfortune, together understood the darker side of life. Lily fled from him, hiding in the bushes when he was around. And Maman, in her sensible way, advised Baby to be cautious. Little Baby had made up her own mind. She thought he was awful and avoided him at every turn.

Katy decided to make the best of things with Monsieur Kupfer.

Caramel was still officially living with Malika, although visiting daily. It was about the time I'd made the contract with her and Violette regarding the food. She assured me that any friend of mine was of course a friend of hers. But if I wanted her personal view, she didn't care for him.

Katy decided to make the best of things with Monsieur Kupfer. She and he were, after all, two French people. She was practical. She was intelligent. She would find ways.

Monsieur Kupfer then decided he wanted to grow strawberries, then he wanted to plant borders of lavender round trees and bushes in the gravelled area.

I agreed to both projects with the idea of keeping him busy and happy. To this day, I don't know whether all these plans were meant to provoke or whether they were serious whims of his disturbed mind.

We bought expensive strawberry plants at the market and a local nursery. He planted them badly in the wrong position on a shallow rim of earth, beside a water channel. Marcelle tried to advise him, at which he threw down his spade and marched off, sulking like a child.

When it came to the lavender bushes, after planting one or two quite inadequately, he suddenly announced that the ground was too hard and he was fed up. He retired angrily to the little house.

Some hours later I went to see him. I found him replying to a large series of advertisements from a marriage bureau and contact magazine. He thought himself a suitable companion for those ladies who demanded cultured, intelligent, lively friends. He already had a pile of letters he'd written on the table beside him, ready to send away. He said he was lonely. He said gardening made him tired. He said the housework, the cooking and the washing and ironing (his own, not mine) made him tired. He needed a woman.

I told him the lavender had been his own idea. If he didn't want to garden, I didn't care. He could just be the *gardien*. But, of course, he wouldn't be paid three hundred francs a week.

He said after all he did want to work in the garden. And then he told me about Lulu.

She was his girlfriend in the north, he said. Lulu didn't live with him. She spent the night occasionally in his house but in the morning she always went back to her own house.

She was divorced, with almost grown-up children who lived with her. One daughter was about to be married. When he'd broached the idea of going south Lulu had said, what a funny thing, that was just what she'd been thinking about. Would she go with him? he'd asked, and she'd said, yes certainly she would, not immediately, but when the time was right—after her daughter's impending marriage for example. When everything was settled she'd follow.

Monsieur Kupfer said one thing worried him. The little house was too small. Lulu had always had her own room even when she'd spent the night at his house. I thought this over. I thought if Monsieur Kupfer couldn't be helpful, perhaps Lulu could. Perhaps she could and would feed the cats, do a little housework, water the flowers on the terrace.

I said to Monsieur Kupfer that, if Lulu would prefer it, I could offer her the little spare room which opened out on to the terrace. Then she'd have her own room.

Monsieur Kupfer wrote to tell Lulu this suggestion, although he continued to write many many letters to women in search of cultivated male friends who liked opera and were good dancers.

'That I am,' said Monsieur Kupfer proudly. 'I am a very good dancer.'

I could believe it. He moved his body deftly and neatly and was light on his feet.

After a long delay—Monsieur Kupfer and I waited anxiously for the post every day—Lulu replied. Monsieur Kupfer showed me her letter. Together we read it several times. She wrote that it was kind of me to offer the room but that, after all, she and Monsieur Kupfer weren't children and when she came they could share the same bedroom.

Monsieur Kupfer was elated. He showed me a photograph of Lulu, a plump, rather plain middle-aged woman with an anxious expression. The weeks went by and there was no sign of Lulu. Her daughter was long married by now, her affairs must be in order.

I realised, finally, that Lulu would never come to join him, that she'd never had any intention of doing so and that she'd sent him away to get rid of him. She hoped that by promising to join him and writing a placating letter every now and then, she'd keep him away. She never wanted to see him again. I asked Monsieur Kupfer a frank question. 'Were you and Lulu lovers?'

'No,' he replied truthfully, but uncomfortably. He had wanted it, but she had not. 'Ah,' I said, deciding the whole relationship was perhaps in his imagination.

Once he realised that Lulu had no intention of joining him, Monsieur Kupfer became more disturbed. There was the affair of the sale of his house in the north. He asked me to help him advertise the house in an English newspaper, because many British people were at that time buying property in Normandy with the advent of the Channel Tunnel. Together we concocted an expensive advertisement for the *Sunday Times* (for which I paid). The house was, he told me, already in the hands of a French agent in the little market town nearest to his village. He showed me a photograph of the house. It looked a fine, large Victorian property, the last house in a village among pine woods.

We had one response to the advertisement. A young Englishman telephoned from London. I gave him the name and telephone number of the local house agent and took the trouble to write to the young man enclosing a copy of the photograph of the house. He didn't reply and that was the last I heard of him.

Long afterwards, long after Monsieur Kupfer had left, his wife telephoned me from Normandy.

Madame Kupfer wanted to know if I had any idea where he might be. I had no idea and didn't want to know. By then, Monsieur Kupfer had involved me in court cases, very expensive and utterly futile.

Madame Kupfer confirmed that he was an ill man with brain damage —and a very unpleasant one. She'd telephoned because he'd suddenly cut off the money from his pension which was due to her. She and their son were in serious difficulties over money.

'Son?'

'Yes—did he never tell you? A fifteen-year-old boy . . .'

'He said he had no children and that he and you were divorced and lived apart . . .'

'Oh no!' She laughed bitterly. 'We're not divorced. We still live together . . .'

'In his house in . . . ?'

I mentioned the name of the village.

'Yes, there. It's my house, partly.'

'But I thought it was for sale.'

'For sale? Certainly not! It's my home.'

'It's not in the hands of a house agent?'

'Oh—that's a part of it. It's divided into two. We have tenants in one part. We thought of selling if the opportunity came up . . . but it's difficult to sell because of the railway line.'

'Railway line?'

'Yes. The trains run along the bottom of the garden—not often, mind you. There aren't that many trains these days—just in the mornings and evenings. But when they go by, it's noisy, of course.'

'Madame Kupfer, have you ever heard of somebody called Lulu?'
'Yes.'

She sounded uncomfortable and her voice dropped. 'Yes—I believe there was some woman. Whether there ever was anything . . .'

This conversation took place about two months after Monsieur Kupfer's departure from Mas des Chats.

When Monsieur Kupfer finally realised that Lulu would never join him he was deeply disappointed and angry. His efforts to find a female companion/slave intensified and he took to visiting the Marseillaise, which had been recommended by Marcelle. I had told her about the endless letters that Monsieur Kupfer had sent off in response to the advertised requests of ladies for gentlemen friends. She said, 'That's no way to find a woman. He ought to go to the Marseillaise,' and this I passed on to Monsieur Kupfer.

The Marseillaise was a huge dance hall, bar, brothel, rendezvous for making contact with other lonely human beings—a kind of aircraft hangar with dance floor and non-stop music. Bands played day and night—or perhaps the music was taped, I never enquired. Men and women went there alone or in couples or groups—sometimes just for the fun of it, sometimes to drink, sometimes for sex, sometimes to find friends or mates. Monsieur Kupfer told me that a free drink went with the price of entry; thereafter every drink was very expensive.

Monsieur Kupfer went there and danced. He danced the tango and the foxtrot and he waltzed and I could imagine that he danced well, with dapper, neat footwork and athletic limbs. He kept meeting women and he told me about them. They were cleverer than I was and they disentangled from him as swiftly as possible.

Once, only once, a woman replied to one of his many letters.

She lived in Marseille and came to Arles by train to meet him. But when she got off the train, Monsieur Kupfer found she'd brought her curé with her. They all three decorously had tea in Arles together and there were no further meetings.

His football activities with the schoolboys of the local town also came to a swift end. He had, at first, been taken on as a once-a-week trainer, but he soon quarrelled with those in charge and was taken off the list of teachers, to his chagrin and anger.

During the last month or so of his months with me, he spent most of his time at the Marseillaise. He no longer worked in the garden and he fed no cats. He did feed the white horse Jasmin, punctiliously, morning and evening. But I discovered he gave Jasmin only rotting carrots. I found in the garage boxes and boxes of carrots, some fresh, mostly rotted. Monsieur Kupfer gave Jasmin, sparingly, a few of the rotten ones. For some time I hadn't supervised what he actually gave the horse, although I'd supplied the bread, apples and carrots.

A month before the three months' trial was due to end I told Monsieur Kupfer that unfortunately he wasn't suited to the job and that at the end of the month he must leave. He decided, instead, to take me to court. This must have been a routine performance for him which he'd undertaken many times in the past. He knew the details of French law perfectly. He went and complained to the Prudhomme in Arles— the workers' council, where any person can bring a complaint, however ill-founded, however crazy, however footling. The complaint will then be investigated, both parties having to be represented in court. I never quite understood the basis of Monsieur Kupfer's complaints against me. One, I know, was that I'd signed his insurance certificates in the wrong place on the form; another was, I believe, unfair dismissal. There was a third to do with damages of some kind . . . and compensation . . . I had to employ a lawyer to represent me, a costly business.

The thing dragged on and on. 'Better a bad settlement,' my lawyer said to me, 'than a good case.'

In the end, I paid Monsieur Kupfer a sum of money and a vast amount to the lawyer, and the case was annulled. Back at the Mas, after threatening many times to ruin me, Kupfer left, but he took the keys of the little house with him. So long as he had not given me back the keys, he could claim, if I took over the house, that I'd stolen possessions of his which remained there. The night after he'd gone I went into the house with my sister, who was visiting me. In the bedroom we found a large pile of cardboard boxes which contained great quantities of very expensive linen articles, with lace, hand-made in

Brittany, tablecloths and mats and handkerchiefs, which we instantly realised must have fallen off the back of a lorry. (Early in his employment with me Monsieur Kupfer had given me a present, a small round white lace table-mat, with a label stuck on it, hand-made in Brittany.)

So long as those boxes were there, I dared not change the locks on the door. Nora said, 'Don't worry, he won't leave them there very long. They're too valuable.'

She was right. Twenty-four hours later, they'd gone. All that was left of Monsieur Kupfer's possessions was an ancient, sad, stubby, faded black folding umbrella, found at the back of the cupboard. He had gone, taking with him my blankets, rugs, pillows and various other articles. He didn't reappear, although he was seen, for a while, in the town where he had another job as caretaker to a home for lost or delinquent children. That, of course, didn't last long.

I had the locks changed. He must have gone elsewhere, on further adventures.

I couldn't wholly dislike or despise that terrible rogue. There was something valiant and something fastidious about him. He refused to be defeated by his illness, by Lulu, by the very adverse circumstances of his life. And he had refused to be brutalised by the brutalising and often humiliating conditions of life as a goods train driver on the French railways which he told me about when I asked him from time to time. I remember with what care he arranged the plates and glasses, washed and dried parsley, removed and discarded critically bruised outer leaves of endives, wearing one of my aprons, on the single occasion, early in his employment with me, when he was *maître d'hôtel* at a lunch party. He was fastidious too, feminine almost, in the care he took of his clothes and his appearance. He put up a system of signals on the narrow road leading to Mas des Chats, using canes and paint and rags to warn drivers of sharp turns and dangerous approaches. And he fenced the little bridge over the canal.

He gave Monsieur le Gris his name and he really did love—or at least feel strongly for—strange Lulu. He also tried to make water run uphill to water a row of irises, digging a channel day after day without, of course, success. His favourite expression after he'd organised things to his satisfaction was '*Comme ça, on est tranquille.*' That was Kupfer.

31

◇

After Kupfer, I decided to do without a *gardien*.

Instead, friends came from England every now and then, stayed a little while and helped to look after animals and house.

The cats objected strenuously, apart from Bruno and Rosie.

Bruno liked company and was polite. Rosie at least behaved sensibly without being enthusiastic. She tried to persuade Lily she needn't act so hysterically.

Why did Lily have to run under beds? They were unlikely to do her harm.

This Lily wouldn't accept. She knew better, she told Rosie. She was convinced that human beings were out to trap her. Then they'd torture her. Then they'd kill her. In laboratories. Hadn't Rosie heard of all this? It was called Science.

Rosie listened carefully. She tried to reassure Lily. She'd heard of all the things Lily had mentioned but in her view it was unlikely to happen at Mas des Chats. She thought I wouldn't allow it.

Lily wasn't persuaded. She was not prepared to trust anyone and she wasn't taking any risks.

So under the bed she went in the small guest room and came out only when the guests had retired to their little house.

In the summer the visitors and I lived out of doors. The shade in the garden was deep and cool. There was an old wild mulberry tree with spreading branches which produced thin, sweet fruit. There were two great plane trees. There was a strange, unusual maple with flowers made of purple silk tassels. In the centre of the lawn was a tall *micocoulier*, a lotus tree. The lotus had a fruit which the magpies and other birds loved to eat in the winter—a fruit mentioned by Homer in the *Odyssey*. Those who eat it, he said, fall into a state of dreamy forgetfulness—thus the 'lotus eaters' who, in the *Odyssey*, had no wish to return home.

At Mas des Chats, unlike the lotus eaters, we were often energetic, taking long walks and drives.

With those who'd never been in Provence before I went to the places

At Mas des Chats we were often energetic, taking long walks and drives along roads whose verges were bright with wild flowers.

which tourists usually visit—Greek and Roman remains, amphitheatres, arches, bridges, aqueducts, excavations. I took them also to medieval monasteries, ancient chapels and to hilltops with exceptionally beautiful views.

We went to Avignon, to Aix en Provence and to Arles.

Arles welcomes travellers with a series of notices, poetic and evocative, on raised placards at the entrance to the town, which mingle with advertisements for petrol, kitchen equipment, furniture and food.

The notices begin '*Arles, ville fleurie*' and then '*Cette route vous conduit à moi, Arles*', followed by '*Je suis l'organisatrice, la Romaine*' and '*Arles, lieux de rencontres*' and finally '*Je suis l'élan, la Mediaevale*'.

I liked to walk up to the church at the top of the old town and look across the roofs of grey and russet tiles to the Rhône and far beyond, where, in the haze, rose the Cevennes.

In the Abbey of Montmajour, nearby, we saw by chance a slow and touching performance of a medieval dance. In the great hall of the monastery, a slender girl moved stiffly to music played on a piano by another girl, both dwarfed to insignificance under the vast stone walls and huge vaulted roof. The music tinkled, the dancer moved like a doll, repeating gestures over and over again. We drifted away.

One of my favourite excursions was to the Gallo-Roman aqueduct and mills at Barbegal. Often deserted, the old stones lay among olive trees and wild fields. There, nightingales sang in the spring in an olive grove beside the aqueduct. And once, looking down the hillside to the Roman mills I heard a cuckoo call and call, the cry growing gradually fainter and fainter and vanishing, as the bird flew northwards.

Coming back to the car we found the locks smashed by would-be thieves. They were mended that evening, only to be broken again next day as the car stood on the heights of the Alpilles while we walked with Caramel. This time a window was also broken. There was nothing to steal in the car either time. I had to report these break-ins to the police for insurance claims. In Arles first, and then St Remy, bored policemen typed the details in triplicate on to sheets of paper, white, yellow and green, without a comment. Car thefts were their daily routine. In St Remy, the policeman had a dark red rose in a small vase on his desk. He handed it to me to smell. The scent was intense.

'The first rose of the season,' he said.

'From your garden?'

'No—here.'

He jerked his head in the direction of the courtyard outside the *gendarmerie*.

Handing me the yellow page of his typewriting he smiled placatingly.

'We can do nothing,' he said. 'No means. Not enough money.'

He shrugged and shook me by the hand.

In the late afternoon we returned to Mas des Chats and swam in the green pool.

Later, when it was quite dark, we ate dinner in the garden.

If there were several people, we sat at a huge stone table which

Monsieur and Madame Belmond had ordered from a local stonemason and had placed on the gravel under the mulberry tree and one of the planes. The table was lit by little candles in glass shades. We felt relaxed and free in the warm night air. Crickets shrilled and the cicadas rasped and the frogs called and the dizzying stars whirled overhead. We drank the wine of the Rhône vineyards and became excited, sun-browned faces flushing in the uneven candlelight.

Magic was distilled from the air—old Provençal magic—and we sipped it, delicately. Life then seemed strange and enchanting.

The hidden cats watched from afar. When the last guest had disappeared they emerged. It was their turn at last. Would I kindly give them their supper? They were famished.

32

Evening. I hear Bruno's falsetto howl, his 'Ladies from Hell' screams on the terrace outside.

Consternation in the kitchen. Lily runs under the table, Oedipussy runs upstairs, Rosie runs, but quickly returns to her place. And Baby takes refuge on the mantelpiece.

I go out and find a large ginger tom facing Bruno squarely and calmly.

They've taken up positions near the syringa bushes. The ginger cat is unmoved by Bruno's hunched back with the hair standing on end. I can see he's indifferent to Bruno's threatening shrieks and his sideways gait. He sits there, provocative and unshaken.

But when I appear he quickly runs to the cypress hedge and then, as I chase him, he goes angrily to the vineyard. Meanwhile, Lily has come outside. She stations herself discreetly on the terrace staring in the direction from which the ginger tom will inevitably return to eat from the cat bowls by the bridge. He appears. She watches him, tender and nervous Lily, who usually has the vapours at the sight of a stranger.

Ginger walks in a dignified way to the dishes of food. Bruno has retired to the kitchen; Lily watches the red cat as he eats slowly and, satisfied, slowly returns to sit by the lavender under the farthest olive tree.

Lily watches him, a steady stare which he returns.

Something is developing between them, a magnetic interchange, some recognition of ancient ties, some affinity which perhaps goes back a million years or more—red cat and white cat, white to red.

Does he remind her of Mews? After a while, he goes away.

He came again, the ginger tom—and again. Once he'd discovered that there was food to be had of an evening at Mas des Chats, he became a regular visitor. Madame Corbet, watching as usual at her window where she had a good view of all who came and went, saw him travelling determinedly down the narrow white lane which led from the main road, sinuously keeping to the bushes. When he arrived, he ate and then strode arrogantly about the terrace, before sitting down in the shade of the old olive tree. Bruno howled and danced with rage, but the ginger tom was indifferent to him. Lily always placed herself somewhere near and stared fixedly at this marvellous stranger. Slowly he turned his head and slowly returned the stare. Then, after a while, he went away.

Le grand chat roux, Madame Corbet called him—and he certainly was very big and strong.

Madame Corbet discovered, from a gossipy neighbour, that he belonged to a couple who had a tumbledown old house on the road to Les Baux but they didn't take any care of him—couldn't be bothered with him, the neighbour had said, and scarcely fed him. Nevertheless, he always went back to that old house and must have regarded it as his home.

Madame Corbet looked on *le grand chat roux* with compassion.

Like Lily, I became attached to him. After he'd eaten with us for a while his coat, previously matted and rough, became thick and shiny. He was a fine cat. Then an epidemic of cat 'flu raged among the outside cats. Some died. The cats of the inner circle were protected from the illness by vaccination.

For a while the ginger tom wasn't seen at Mas des Chats. When he came again it was clear he was ill. He had become thinner. His coat was shabby and dirty. A brown exudate blocked his nostrils. But he ate hungrily. Then, without swaggering on the terrace, he went quickly away.

A week passed, during which he failed to attend the evening meal. Then, one afternoon, I was walking along the vineyard when a thin and shrunken ginger cat staggered towards me from out of the bushes and rubbed himself against my legs, touchingly, pathetically. I could hardly recognise *le grand chat roux*, hardly believe it was he.

I fed him with the most nourishing food I had and gave him milk and cream. He ate and drank, then disappeared. It was a few days later that I went into one of the spare rooms upstairs where things were stored and ironing was done. There was an old but comfortable cat basket in the room. In it, I saw with a shock the emaciated ginger tom, curled up, unmoving, suffering terribly. He had come to us to die.

Lily didn't seem to notice that the ginger tom had gone. She went on with her songs and her flowers and her little strange squeaks of pleasure as if nothing had happened.

I telephoned at once to the veterinary clinic. The young vet quickly came. *Le grand chat roux* was helped out of his incurable illness to a peaceful death.

Lily didn't seem to notice that he'd gone. She went on with her songs and her flowers and her little strange squeaks of greeting and pleasure as if nothing had happened.

Only I was sad for him—and Madame Corbet—a little.

33

Monsieur and Madame Belmond had enclosed the area of the swimming pool with a fence made of rushes. Perhaps they liked to swim naked, floating weightless and amorous over the boy with the dolphins. They probably felt more secure with the fence, but the pool was in any case secluded. The Mas des Chats itself was secret, unexpected, hidden in the fields at the end of a small, remote road. I had the rush fence removed on the southern side of the pool where a row of cypresses stood. Beyond them was the vineyard. Swimming in the pool, I could then see the green vines and, in the distance, the blue Alpilles. On the northern side of the pool was another row of cypresses, oleanders with flowers of yellow and red and a great pomegranate bush. The pomegranates were wild, not good to eat, but the birds enjoyed the rosy fruit and the flowers were charming.

Beyond the cypresses was the garden, green and cool with large trees, and the terrace. Many pots and jars of geraniums stood there, and ferns and arum lily and a lemon tree.

In the hot weather I liked to swim in the late afternoon and the cats rose up from their various siestas in the shade to join me. They stretched and yawned, then strolled slowly to take up positions around the pool to watch me.

I could imagine their wishful dreams as they slept through the heat of the afternoon.

Maman might have dreamed she was back in the farmhouse kitchen, sitting on the lap of that loved person whom she'd lost before she made her way to Mas des Chats.

Baby might have dreamed that she and Bruno had eloped to a far country where mice grew on trees.

Hélène would have dreamed that all the cats except Oedipus and Emilie had disappeared. She was left in possession of Mas des Chats, Queen of her territory and much loved and prized by me.

Rosie might have dreamed she was the headmistress of a good girls' school and that she was giving the sixth form a lecture on Darwin. Lily might have dreamed she was drifting across green grass in fine warm

What did they dream of, Hélène and Oedipus, as they slept through the heat of the afternoon?

rain and Nancy's Mum was there with a nice fresh piece of coley and a bottle of Hampshire milk. Nero would have dreamed he'd found a rabbit on the lawn.

Ocdipus would have dreamed he was alone on an island with a beautiful female cat who loved him as much as his mother did.

Katy would have dreamed Monsieur le Gris was dead.

Monsieur le Gris would have dreamed he was Boss cat and had the bed to himself and that Bruno was his second-in-command.

And Bruno might have dreamed that someone had given him a

magician's hat and wand and that all the other cats sat round him spellbound while he amazed them with trick after trick.

And I might have dreamed—what? Life at Mas des Chats was in any case often like a dream. In the warm late afternoon, drifting in the deep green water of the pool, looking at the sunlight slanting on the sharp bright leaves of the vines with the blue hills beyond—the ten beautiful cats in attendance—who would wish for a better moment?

I scattered the wide terrace with pots of flowering plants.

In summer the fields were brilliant with sunflowers.

Nero, a fine, dignified cat with gleaming coat and golden eyes.

Timid Monsieur le Gris grew into a heavy barrel of a cat, but remained at heart a baby.

Elegant and courageous, Hélène was a devoted mother.

Katy, constantly bullied by the other cats, was an enthusiastic walker.

Monsieur le Gris and Oedipus became deeply attached to one another.

The little dog Caramel had a beautiful nature and lovely eyes.

34

—◇—

Katy was often in trouble and often in need of rescue. She hid in cupboards and so was shut in on several occasions. She managed to get herself locked in the garage and imprisoned in the room where the water tanks and furnace were installed.

On one occasion she was stranded on the roof of the house. She'd reached the roof by climbing a tall pine tree which rose up about a metre from the wall and roof. It was easy enough for a cat to jump from tree to roof—not so easy to jump from roof to tree. It needed courage and a sure footing. Monsieur le Gris could do it with ease—and march into the kitchen brushing the resin from his paws. But he was a cat of exceptional strength and agility in spite of his weight. Katy, on the roof, had lost her nerve. She marched up and down, crying. I tried to show her an alternative route down by the sloping roofs of the guest rooms. But she refused this and went on tramping from one end of the tiles to the other, wailing in her thin, shrill little voice.

Rosie, staring up, intimated to me that if she were in my place, she'd leave Katy there and not bother to rescue her.

The other cats also gazed up at her and passed their secret judgements.

In the end, towards evening, I telephoned for the *pompiers* who were trained for the rescue of cats from roofs—and from wells, they told me—as part of their normal duties. Just as the fire engine noisily arrived, Katy appeared in the kitchen.

The two young firemen accepted my apology and 200 francs very cheerfully and went away again.

Katy sat down and began to clean her coat—nonchalantly.

But all that was before she had an accident that maimed her for life.

She had the very bad habit of hiding under cars, moving away only as the engine started. One day I found her lying in a chair in the dining-room in great pain. The knee joint of her left hind leg had been crushed, presumably by a car.

I took her at once to the clinic, where she was anaesthetised and

The *pompiers* included rescuing cats from roofs as part of their training, as well as their normal fire-fighting duties.

the wound cleaned and strapped. Once so agile, so quick and elegant in her movements, poor Katy now was awkward. The wound healed, the strapping was removed but the joint was forever stiff and sometimes painful. Katy became fearful. She dared not risk an encounter with Monsieur le Gris or another aggressive cat. Sad little black and white cat, she hid in holes and a wood pile and seemed to have no place she felt was her own special territory.

Then I took a hand and installed her in the salon. After a while she

Katy found she could fit herself into a large pottery jar in the salon. There she spent many hours, every day, feeling secure.

made herself very comfortable. There she felt safe, for I shut her in so that Monsieur le Gris, hurling himself against the windows, couldn't disturb her. She found she could fit herself into a large pottery jar. There she spent many hours, every day, feeling secure, like Ali Baba —or Diogenes.

Gradually her leg recovered. But she was never again quite so nimble, so like quicksilver, as before her accident.

35

Rosie, rushing into the house in a lull of the storm, shaking rivulets of water from her coat, complained bitterly about the violence of the weather—uncivilised, she thought, like so much else in France. She shuddered and darted under a chair as another fierce flash of lightning ripped at the sky, followed immediately by a ferocious crash of thunder.

Lily, who had long taken refuge under a low table, joined in with a small squeak as the thunder rolled. How different from the rain in England, she implied, and reminded me how she had loved the rain in England.

'You may think you loved it, dear Lily,' I said, 'many's the time I had to rescue you from under the tree peony, soaking wet, too nervous to cross the lawn.'

Lily, squeaking again with a new crash of thunder, claimed that she hadn't asked me to bring her in from under the tree peony. I had insisted. She'd been enjoying the smell of wet grass, damp leaves, drops of water hanging from the branches, soft earth . . .

'Come on, Lily and Rosie,' I said, 'stop making such a fuss. The rain here is often just the same as in England . . .'

The rain in my part of Provence came from the south, from the sea —the real rain, that is. There might be a scattering of mean, cold raindrops from the north-west when the Tramontane was blowing, that hard, unkind cold wind that filled the sky with grey clouds and was the very breath of winter. But rain that fell warmly and solidly, that might last for two or three days, was brought by sea winds. This rain might arrive slowly. Clouds gathered gradually, usually in still, windless weather. They came softly over the Alpilles, bringing first the smell of rain. The land waited. The pine trees on the hills waited. A little rain fell, then more, until at last there was a steady downpour. Vapoury mist formed on the tops of the Alpilles, blotting out the shapes of hills. Sometimes the clouds had gathered first over the Sahara. The rain was red, the colour of mud, the colour of ochre, the sands of the desert drawn up into the sky.

The cats came, one by one, reluctantly indoors, shaking water from their coats. If the rain fell for a few days without a break, the bored cats became very restive and irritable with one another and the litter boxes were overused. After a hot dry spell, water was, of course, a boon for the parched land.

One day, when Caramel and I walked in fine rain among the orchards, we met an old farmer who growled at me defiantly, '*Il fait beau!*' and added more amiably, '*Beau pour la terre!*' rumbling over the last syllable like a roll of thunder.

36

I made friends in Provence, as time went on. They were mostly English or North American, but there were also some French among them. One woman was a Professor of Anthropology at an American university, a well-known writer and broadcaster.

She had a house not far from mine where she spent holidays, or sometimes came to write her books. She was perfectly sane and very intelligent. I mention this because of a conversation we once had. She telephoned to invite me to dinner. Then she added, rather nervously, 'I've had a strange day. I've been obsessed by moths . . .'

'Moths?'

'This morning I thought I saw a moth in my bedroom. I put on my glasses to see it better. It was a moth, I thought. I had a sudden image of moths invading every closet and eating my clothes when I'm away. I took two aerosols of insecticide and emptied them into all the cupboards in the house. Then I thought that's that and went into Avignon. But suddenly I began thinking of the moths again. I saw the whole house being destroyed by moths—curtains, carpets, upholstery. I had to come home—but first I bought a ton of moth balls and then I started putting them everywhere, all over the house. I imagined I could see moth holes wherever I looked . . .'

I laughed.

'I understand how you feel. D'you think we'd be affected in the same way if we saw a moth in central London?'

'No, not in central anywhere. This could only happen in Provence —this fear that one's about to be overwhelmed—and consumed—by moths—or whatever . . .'

'Why d'you think it happens here?'

'The harsh climate. I think it's the harsh climate . . .'

It was true that the land in our corner of Provence often seemed to be holding its breath, waiting for some catastrophic blow from the weather—violent rain and storms, searing heat, frost, drought, lightning, the Mistral, forest fires. The landscape itself was disturbing, even agitating at times—never mild and gentle like the English wooded hills at Ashford, smoothed over by mist and soft rain. There was tension and drama in Provence, seeming to be inherent in the land. Sometimes the beauty was so intense, the light so pure and brilliant, to look was almost unbearable. Sometimes I couldn't look long enough. In spring and summer the richness could hardly be encompassed by human vision. Under the burning blue of the sky, the bright grass shone and the midnight cypresses marched across the valley, interspersed with rows of tall, feathery poplars. Then there were the orchards of grey-green olive trees and, in the distance, always the lavender shapes of the hills.

The land vibrated with the shrilling of crickets and the cicadas' dry, repetitive buzz, and at night the stars whirled and the moon cut the sky like a knife and green light lay along the horizon, still stained with sunset pink, and the frogs shouted.

When the Mistral blew strongly, every tree, every blade of grass, the cornfields and the poppies and sunflowers and the yellow fields of rape were possessed, thrown into ripples and waves of savage dance. Some, like me, became taut and highly strung. So also Jeanne, who could feel seriously threatened by moths.

But it was more than the weather, I thought, that gave rise to madness in Provence.

37

My ten beautiful cats took life composedly. Apart from Rosie, that is. She enjoyed injecting a little drama into the scene. And would incite the others, so that hysteria sometimes reigned around her. If ever there was a sudden crisis, a scattering and jumping and crying of cats, I could be sure Rosie was at the bottom of it. When all the cats had finally settled for the night, Rosie would happily create a disturbance by galloping noisily along the corridor and thundering out into the night. Because I had forbidden and prevented her from taking it out on Katy, she focused instead on Oedipus. One evening she caused an uproar by leaping suddenly and furiously on Oedipus who was dozing comfortably on the spare room bed. Oedipus screamed and rushed under the bed. Lily roused herself anxiously from her sleep on a mat in the corridor. Monsieur le Gris came out of the *bibliothèque* to see what was going on and so ran into Bruno who, on hearing Oedipus scream, had hurried to Rosie's aid. Monsieur le Gris refused to give way to Bruno, growling and grumbling in his throat. Bruno rushed to use his litter box noisily and threateningly, then began to howl, so causing le Gris great disquiet.

Rosie, her thick tail erect, felt very pleased with herself. She'd dispatched that upstart from God knows where. She marched back into my bedroom where I remonstrated with her.

They had no *right* there, was what she smugly insisted.

At this point, Monsieur le Gris, poor fellow, decided he couldn't tolerate Bruno's thrashing tail and glaring blue eyes a moment longer, so made his humiliated way downstairs. Bruno returned to the bedroom and jumped on the bed beside Rosie.

She gave a deep sigh of satisfaction and, purring gently, pleased at having got rid of the rabble, she composed herself for a peaceful sleep. Bruno gave her a few gentle licks on her forehead and she closed her great eyes with a contented little squeak.

But when Rosie chose to be charming, she excelled. She was particularly fond of my sister who visited once a year. Rosie haunted her room. She supervised the unpacking of the suitcase and the storing of

Oedipus had a large head, with huge intelligent green eyes. Despite his beauty, he became a regular target for Rosie's aggression.

the clothes in cupboards. She enjoyed what Nora called Drawer Work, climbing from drawer to drawer and investigating the contents with scrupulous curiosity.

She was also very interested in bed-making, ably assisted by Bruno. They would leap into the middle of the bed and remain there. When they could be persuaded to move, they'd jump on the sheets and pillow slips, making it impossible to pull them in position.

Bruno would try to wrap himself in a sheet or two while Rosie pretended there was a mouse under the blanket. Then they would ask if there was anything more that they could do to help.

Rosie also had her sentimental moments and her moments of weakness. She would sit on my lap and bury her head under my arm, asking to be stroked and reassured. She was meltingly sweet at those times, just a gentle little English cat, without an unkind thought in her head.

38

One day we found Jasmin's field empty. He'd gone. We discovered later he'd been sold by Monsieur Mabeille to his brother, the shepherd, who already had two Camargue horses in a stable somewhere among the huddle of farm buildings and houses. I had seen those two horses who had nothing to do all day but eat and were as round as barrels. At least Jasmin would have shelter from the winter winds and enough to eat. Monsieur Mabeille received a piece of a tractor in return for the horse. I was invited by the shepherd's wife to visit Jasmin, but I never went and then I heard he'd been sold again.

I pray and hope his new owners were kind and caring of him.

We, the cats and I, used to go and look at Jasmin's empty field which had a lonely and deserted air. Weeds grew high and the stream where he drank was blocked by fallen leaves and rotting branches. We missed him, mysterious white wild animal from the Camargue.

Although we hardly knew him, we sensed his serious, determined approach to life, his stoic endurance and a certain sweetness of character.

39

Only two roads crossed the Alpilles from north to south, winding among the rocks and pines, twisting and turning like snakes. At their highest points two giant posters urged passers-by to protect the forests from fire. 'The forests enhance life!' shouted the posters. 'Let us save them! Save the forests!'

Lower down on the hills in thickly wooded areas, sharp red notices warned '*Zone Rouge*', forbidding walkers to enter the woods. In places, during the summer months, smoking was prohibited and the lighting of camp fires was a crime. Chains prevented cars from travelling the gravel contour paths which were reserved for fire engines and fire fighters. Underground stores of water were placed at strategic points along these roads, and day and night firemen watched on the hilltops for signs of smoke or fire.

In spite of all these precautions, each summer brought a series of terrible fires which usually broke out when the Mistral was blowing strongly. Fire engines from villages miles around, hurriedly enlisted fire-fighters, the Canadair, small water-carrying planes—none of these prevented hundreds of acres of pine woods and *garrigue* being destroyed with all their wildlife. Afterwards, for many months there was a desolate moon landscape of grey ash and blackened tree stumps.

One summer at Mas des Chats we had our own fire. In the farmland and woods surrounding the towns and villages, the communes imposed strict rules about the lighting of fires. In summer agricultural debris had to be burnt before 10 a.m. and all fires extinguished after that hour. No fires were to be lit at all when the Mistral blew. The fires must be far from the *garrigue* and water must always be at hand to extinguish them.

All this the local inhabitants knew very well. That didn't prevent my excellent gardener Monsieur Mercier from setting alight the countryside around Mas des Chats.

One morning, sitting at a late breakfast with Nora who was paying a summer visit, we heard the sirens howl.

'What is that?' asked Nora.

'A fire somewhere, perhaps. Police—an accident . . .'

I had just been congratulating myself on the general calm and a sense of things being under control and was in a tranquil mood.

The sirens sounded uncomfortably close. We went out to investigate. Thick clouds of smoke billowed upwards from the surrounding fields. Beyond the vineyard lay a blackened landscape and, half obscured by Mistral-driven smoke, little soot-stained figures ran hither and thither carrying hoses. Here and there was the vague red shape of a fire engine—the whole scene like an incoherent nightmare.

Monsieur Mercier, wishing to lead water along a little canal blocked by clippings from the vines, had decided the quickest way to clear the waterway was by burning the clippings. He had set light to two bonfires simultaneously. The sparks, leaping up in the wind, had instantly set fire to the tangle of dry grass and vegetation in the fields around us.

Blown by the Mistral, the fire had raced forwards to reach the main road. On the edge of this road were gathered all the neighbours and many passers-by to watch the fun. Then the police turned up and not long afterwards the firemen contained the fire, although smouldering patches remained.

As soon as I appeared, a deputation of men, women and children, members of a large family who owned many hectares in the neighbourhood, including one of those burned by Monsieur Mercier, hurried to greet me.

'My trees!' began the leader of the deputation, Monsieur Gondron. He pointed threateningly to a row of blackish cypresses, damaged by the fire, certainly, but many had been dead long before the fire raced through them. 'My melons!' he went on to say. 'My melons will be damaged, having no shelter from the wind.'

I looked in astonishment at the field which lay beyond the trees. No melons grew there. It was full of old cabbage leaves, old fruit boxes, old plastic bags, stones and weeds.

'Melons?'

'Yes, I have a plan to grow melons on that spot. They'd have difficulty,' he said, 'surviving without shelter.'

Melons, in fact, don't need to be sheltered from the wind here. In any case, many of the trees were still alive.

The police also played a rôle in this surrealistic drama. A young policeman with walkie-talkie and notebook scribbled on a page and told me Monsieur Mercier had committed a felony of the fourth order. Having taken my name, he told me I would later be called to the *gendarmerie* to make a full statement.

Monsieur Mercier stood silent and downcast on the edge of the vineyard cursing himself for his stupidity. Though in the event no real damage was done, there could have been a serious disaster.

'You know, it *says* something about him that he could do that,' said my friend the psychoanalyst. 'It *means* something . . .'

'I know. I know what it means. Monsieur Mercier is a man of inner violence. He's only happy when he's cutting and chopping . . . and now, this . . . But he's a marvellous gardener . . .'

When the fire had been completely subdued and the fire engines, firemen, police and bystanders had gone away, the beautiful cats walked out to see what had become of their fields.

They sniffed the blackened grass and charred earth in astonishment. Bruno and the others couldn't understand the change in the landscape from one day to the next.

My insurance company was asked to pay the farmer a certain sum for limited damage to a few cypress trees.

I spent a long morning at the police station with Caramel. I was summoned to be there at 10.30. The policeman at the desk gave me a chair and sat me down beside him. Many people came and went with their problems and anxieties. Women made complaints about the behaviour of their husbands. Men complained about their wives. The young policeman consulted a book on the law and gave what advice he could. Teams of police, sometimes in uniform, sometimes in plain clothes, drifted in from other stations. They talked about their holidays or their plans for the future. Once a long conversation developed about the fan in the ceiling, idly revolving above us. Motorists came in and reported break-ins on their cars. Then a surly man with his hands handcuffed behind him was ushered in by a little crowd of plain clothes police and hurried to the cells. In between incidents, the policeman gave some of his attention to me. Together we constructed a ten-line statement on the origin of the fire, the damage done and the character of Monsieur Mercier. Caramel became restive. Various passing policemen patted her. At last we were released.

The incident was over.

The great forest fires continued to break out, exhausting the men who fought them, exhausting the pilots of the Canadair.

They would go on doing so every summer.

Monsieur Mercier was never called to the courts or made to pay a fine. Monsieur Gondron, on the other hand, was made to clean up his patch of rubbish beyond the trees where he'd dreamed of planting melons.

Afterwards, I thought deeply about Monsieur Mercier's behaviour. It was always confusing to find in him a juxtaposition of violence and gentleness—extreme roughness and extreme courtesy. When working in the garden he was habitually immensely quick and impatient—yet he would stay long after his hours were done, discussing with me, and enjoying doing so, almost every plant and shrub, every plan he had in mind for improvement. When Nora brought him a small Armenian plate from her travels he was deeply moved. He made a speech of thanks worthy of a troubadour or a gentleman at the court of Louis XIV, so graceful and articulate and charming it was. On the other hand he appeared to feel great satisfaction when savaging trees and shrubs with a reckless saw, uprooting and throwing away pretty plants because he regarded them as untidy, flooding the grass and flowerbeds with a destructive surge of water from the canal.

Was this schism in his character typically French or peculiar to him, an outcome of the split in his childhood affections?

40

Not long after the fire at Mas des Chats, the drought was broken by heavy storms.

Nora was nearing the end of her visit when we drove to the hill town of Uzès to have dinner with friends—an hour away. As we left the Mas, large drops of rain began to fall. Dark clouds were massing in the sky, covering a bright moon. On the journey, rain fell heavily in places. But while we were in Uzès, the storm clouds drifted away to the north.

At midnight, we returned. The roads were wet, with here and there black pools of treacherous water—but now the moon shone out of a clearing sky.

Not far from Mas des Chats we found gravel in quantity on the road and lumps of tarmac and débris. Driving became difficult. It was necessary to do a kind of slalom around the rocks or large branches torn from trees which were strewn across the roads.

When we reached our own gravel road leading to the Mas, I thought I'd taken the wrong turning. The road was unrecognisable, almost impassable. A violent torrent of water rushing down from the Alpilles had torn great caves in the surface. Large stones lay here and there together with branches and clumps of green leaves. A ferocious purely local storm must have broken over Mas des Chats and its surroundings. We drove apprehensively down the transformed lane.

Mas des Chats was in darkness. Lightning overhead had caused the power switch to jump.

There was a small lake by the car shelter. What was the state of the beautiful cats? I reset the power switch and the lights came on.

We found ten sober, nervous and reproachful cats, some with very wet coats, sheltering in the kitchen. A few, like Lily and Hélène, lay under tables and chairs. Others more brave sat on top of the furniture. We greeted them with relief.

The telephone rang—Madame Corbet, the neighbour. 'The worst storm for twenty years,' she said. Her kitchen was knee-deep in water. Were we all right?

Luckily we were.

The cats, licking their coats, gathered round, seeming to be amazed that we could possibly have left them in those circumstances.

'We didn't know,' we said.

'What will happen next?' asked Nora.

Laughing a little nervously, we went to our rooms.

Rosie found it hard to believe that, after all that, she wouldn't immediately be given a comforting meal. So I fed her quickly and secretly, hoping the others wouldn't notice, and went to bed.

It cost three thousand francs to repair the road surface with a mixture of earth and stones. The bill was divided into four, shared by the owners of the various houses. Mademoiselle Abeille owned three houses on the road, so she should have paid a larger part—but her *teutrice* argued and quibbled on her behalf.

The elderly sister-in-law of Madame Corbet was the last to pay. She owned the house in which the Arab-Spanish family lived. As they hadn't paid the rent for some time she was reluctant to improve the road for their use. In the end she did pay. She sent a letter with her cheque, written by her daughter and signed by her in a quavery hand. In it she told me how reluctant she was to pay her share. 'My tenants don't pay me my rent. *Je vous prie de croire que ce n'est pas de gaité de coeur* that I have expenses on their account.'

I understood very well how she felt and so did Caramel.

41

Rosie and Lily complained repeatedly about the milk in Provence. One sip and they turned away, claiming the milk was old and tired and tasted of cardboard, not at all the clean fresh drink they'd enjoyed at Ashford.

I agreed with them. The milk came down from the north of France packed in cardboard boxes, together with the butter and cheeses and yoghurt and cream, on a journey that might take days. There were only goats, no cows, in Provence. The farmers around Mas des Chats never drank cows' milk. Madame Corbet sometimes sipped, delicately, a cup of hot water in which reposed a modest Lyons' tea bag, but she'd never dream of adding milk or even lemon.

Rosie and Lily, giving up all ideas of fresh cows' milk, agreed to settle for a tablespoon of UHT *crème longue durée* with a little warm water in it. The rest of the indoor cats, learning quickly, followed suit. But the less spoiled cats drank the cardboard packaged milk with enjoyment.

I understood, watching my cats and Caramel, that food represented security as well as something to stave off hunger or a delightful pastime.

When there was an invasion of neighbourhood cats in the garden, as happened from time to time—starving cats, desperate for food— my cats needed reassurance. Nero and Monsieur le Gris and also Oedipus would come into the kitchen time after time saying they were hungry. But after they'd nibbled a few mouthfuls, they'd go outside again. Monsieur le Gris, if he wasn't hungry enough to eat at all, went through the motions of scratching the kitchen floor, solemnly trying to cover his dish with symbolic earth. He did, in fact, do his best, very often, to bury the dishes I'd put out for neighbourhood cats in the garden beds. I'd find them dusted with earth and old leaves. 'Atavism,' I said reproachfully.

Monsieur le Gris gazed at me with lofty disapproval. This was one of the few subjects on which he agreed with Rosie. Like her, he believed that an invasion of strange cats would be the ruin of the cat

Monsieur le Gris would come into the kitchen from time to time claiming that he was hungry, but would go outside again after nibbling a few mouthfuls.

Katy was the last to come in for her supper. She waited until she was sure there'd be no competition and no arguments.

community at Mas des Chats. There would be stealing of food and beds and worse—leading to anarchy and a decline of civilisation.

He padded majestically from the kitchen, solid grey tub of a cat, glaring meaningfully at me with his beautiful eyes, round and yellow and black.

And his parting shot, delivered with a scathing backward glance, was to remind me that by now I should have known that he didn't care for Kit-e-Kat *au boeuf*.

Katy was the last to come in for her supper. She waited until she was sure there'd be no competition and no arguments. Jumping on the counter by the sink, she'd begin by asking, in typically French manner, what was on the menu. Then she'd discuss the various possibilities, asking whether this was good or that was fresh. She'd eat with great enjoyment and great discrimination, small amounts at a time. If the ambience wasn't right she'd run out without eating and come back when she reckoned things had improved. She ate a little of this and a little of that, seeming to comment as she went along, '*Ah! C'est bon!*' or 'I've known better' or 'Not entirely fresh' or '*délicieux*' or 'I prefer the Sheba, but as this is here I'll have a little.' Occasionally she sent her compliments to the chef, but on the whole her tone was critical. Smallest and lightest of the cats, small and light she remained.

42

Caramel had a beautiful nature and lovely eyes, as people were always telling me. She was usually cheerful and lively and never sulked even in bad times. But sometimes her face had the look of a very old dog —a dog who'd known all the suffering that in this world a little dog may know. The look was weary and sad and made me try to comfort her.

Most of the time Caramel seemed eager and happy, doing her best to please. She had become calmer and less possessive as the years went by, although it remained a torment for her to see me making a fuss of one of the cats. She tried to endure this by screwing up her eyes and pretending to sleep.

I did everything possible to help her to feel loved and secure. The daily walk was her great joy. Like many country dogs, she enjoyed the excitement of walks in the little towns where the pavements and street corners were full of marvellous smells. We went to many of the charming old market towns around us—St Remy and Maillane, Mollèges, Egalières and St Etienne du Grès.

Sometimes we went to Tarascon which Caramel particularly enjoyed. She dragged me excitedly along the narrow streets and the wide boulevard towards a promenade near the banks of the Rhône. There, it seemed, there was a public lavatory for all the dogs of the town and there we strolled. I looked at the great river now in the last stage of its journey to the sea, and the pale castles of Beaucaire and Tarascon facing one another across the water.

Caramel looked at the ground and investigated every smell. Occasionally we walked on the Beaucaire side of the Rhône where there was a boat club and a stretch of grass, trees and gravel at the water's edge. Caramel was nervous of the river. I tried to interest her in it and told her I'd seen it in its beginnings in Switzerland in the Valais. She didn't listen. Her look said, 'There's too much water here. I'd rather go somewhere else.'

Sometimes we went to Les Baux, perched on its high hill among cliffs and precipices of white stone. One winter evening, when the town was deserted, we drove up to walk along the ramparts. I left the car in the empty parking lot, and as Caramel and I entered the cobbled streets an attendant lurched out of his warm hut.

'Madame,' he called, *'dix francs pour le parking!'*

Difficult to believe—but ten francs it was or else leave the car a long way down the road and walk back. Winter and summer, Les Baux was floodlit at night. The old town floated eerily against the stars, glimpsed every now and then from a curve in the mountain road. Down in the valley, lights twinkled, expensive restaurants and rich men's houses.

43

Maurice, the one-eyed cat who belonged, as Caramel had done, to the Arab-Spanish neighbours, sometimes found his way into the house on bitterly cold nights. Like the dogs, it was impossible to get rid of him. He was a passive resister, limp and toneless.

He sat like a stone carving on a radiator. He didn't beg, but he hoped desperately that I'd let him stay. I'd thrown him out many times but he came back, silently, like a small dark ghost, one eyed. One night he coughed. His cough sounded to me painfully like the croup of babies I used to care for in the children's wards of big hospitals—a pitiful, croaking cough.

Small figure, dignified, still as stone. I let Maurice stay.

Maurice, my neighbours' one-eyed cat, came regularly for food, and for shelter too on bitterly cold nights.

44

Brilliant had quickly learned that he could expect to find a dish of food put out for him at the back of the house towards evening. Occasionally, however, he turned up in the morning if he was very hungry. He'd lie down, front paws crossed as usual, and wait, staring fixedly at the corner of the house where he hoped to see me appear carrying his dish. Every now and then he'd give a quick, anxious glance at the kitchen window to see if I might be there preparing his food.

In winter, there was a problem. If his dish of food was put out before he turned up to eat it, a flock of magpies would drop out of the sky in moments and gobble it up, leaving hardly a crumb.

If Brilliant then arrived to find his dish empty, he'd come sidling round to the front of the house to the dishes put out for the vagabond cats and lick them clean. If these 'outside' cats found nothing to eat on their plates, they'd steal into the house through the cat window and raid the dishes of the 'indoor' cats.

To prevent the magpies eating Brilliant's food, I had to give them their own food. If Brilliant found his dish full, he wouldn't eat the cats' food and the 'outside' cats would stay outside. So, in order to be sure that all received food, the magpies first had to be satisfied. There were a great many magpies. The hunters didn't shoot them as they weren't edible. They roved about among the cypress hedges, great families of them. I always saluted them when I saw them by the road. 'One for sorrow, two for mirth . . .' but there was seldom one alone.

Although I found the magpies' behaviour over Brilliant's food irritating, adding to the burden of feeding many animals, I very much admired them. They are handsome, intelligent birds. I had a special sympathy for them.

I'd once had a tame magpie. He—or she— died not long before I made the journey to France.

The magpie fell out of its nest as a fledgling. One of the cats heard a rustling of leaves as the little bird hopped among the bushes under a group of tall pines in the garden of Ashford Cottage. I rescued it just as the cat was about to pounce. A small bundle of black and white feathers, even then it seemed friendly and fearless.

What should I do with it?

My previous experience of rescuing infant birds had been depressing. All had died sooner or later in spite of the efforts made to feed and care for them.

Mother birds, or rather parent birds, were, I believed, supposed to rescue their young if they fell from the nest. How this was done I couldn't imagine. The magpie was far too young to fly and its nest must have been almost at the top of a tall pine tree. But I must try to give the parents a chance to rescue it. I placed the magpie high up on a thin branch of one of the pines. It clung there with spindly claws for all it was worth, rocking to and fro as it tried to keep its balance.

If the parent was to arrive, I must disappear—for a while.

I'd hardly crossed the lawn when I heard the fierce cawing of crows. They were dropping down like bomber aircraft on the little magpie. I rushed back to save it. Poor creature, it lay on the ground. One of its fragile legs was broken, one eye pecked to bleeding blindness. My fault!

But I was ignorant of the harm which might be done to it. So much for Nature!

Now, of course, I must see if human care might save it. William placed a tiny splint on the broken leg. I gently bathed its injured eye. The little magpie bravely suffered our attempts to heal it. Its leg mended slowly and was strong. Its eye also healed but was blind. The magpie had to look at the world on her left side by turning and tilting her head.

I say 'her'. We never discovered if the bird were male or female but I felt it had the courage and endurance of a female—and a feminine quality. We named her Pica Pica.

She survived and grew strong. For several months she commuted between London and Hampshire. During the week she lived in a room in a flat overlooking the Marble Arch. At weekends she had a room of her own at Ashford Cottage. In these rooms she was free. She hopped about. She had toys and healthy food and water. She seemed to enjoy her life.

Lily and Rosie tried to destroy her, of course.

I could imagine Rosie haranguing me about Nature and the damage done by interfering with the course of it.

Best to eliminate the weak and feeble, survival only of the fittest. These were the cardinal rules of life, the rules of evolution.

'Rosie,' I said, 'the magpie is charming and intelligent. She is worth saving.' In my view, human beings' great—and perhaps only—contribution to this world was their drive to bypass the rules of evolution:to save the weak and feeble. The laws of evolution were cruel and shocking—offensive to the human sense of right and wrong, of fairness and compassion.

Rosie gave me a baleful look meant to warn me that no good would come of it. The rules were very old and very well tried. They'd worked for millions of years. I had to agree that I and other human beings hadn't even considered the consequences of our sense of right and wrong. What might be right for the individual might be disastrous for the group—and so for future individuals in the group.

'Well—I understand what you say, but I intend to save this magpie if I can, I'd be most grateful if you'd leave her alone.'

They wouldn't leave her alone, of course, Rosie and Lily. They tried to get at Pica at every opportunity, but I was careful to protect her.

She was carried in a cage from house to car and from car to house. Once in her room with the door firmly shut, the cage was opened.

She was charming and affectionate and very clever. She sang, she chattered. She ate her food with great interest, turning her one-eyed head to peer with the good eye at it. On one occasion she even drank a few sips of champagne. She grew large wings and a long tail. Her plumage of white, iridescent green and black was glossy and beautiful. She learned to fly.

Once, before she could fly properly, we nearly lost her.

The woman who came to clean the flat at Marble Arch opened a window in Pica's room just wide enough for her to escape. I was busy seeing patients. Once free, I looked in Pica's room. She had gone. I rushed to the window. There, three stories below me, on the pavement of Stanhope Place, stood Pica, holding court to an admiring crowd. She had coasted down from the window and landed in the street. I fled down the stairs but by the time I arrived in the street, Pica had vanished.

Members of the crowd still lingered. Where was she? Someone had sent for the RSPCA and their van had arrived just as I was tearing down the stairs.

She had been taken to a hostel miles away.

It took nearly two days to recover her. The hostel was open only during hours when I worked.

By the time we fetched her, one member of the staff at the hostel had fallen in love with Pica. She had planned to take her home where she kept another wild bird. She was disappointed that I wanted her back.

Pica seemed happy to see us. She chuckled and sang in the car on the way home and ate her specially delicious welcome-back supper with enthusiasm.

When she was fully grown, it was clearly unkind to keep her in locked rooms—either in London or in the country. By now she could fly. I had a cage constructed for her under a tree in a paved part of the garden at Ashford Cottage. There she had shelter and a series of perches and more space—but not enough. She flew up and down and down and up her cage in a melancholy way. Lily and Rosie prowled around outside thinking that now their time had come to destroy her.

I decided I must find a better way of life for her.

I asked advice all round. The vet, Mr Richards, said, looking at Pica in her cage,

'Let her out. She won't fly off. She'll stay around and be tame. She'll follow you everywhere.'

The gardener said he'd had a tame magpie once when he was a boy. The bird had gone everywhere with him, even into the local town, perched on the handlebars of his bicycle.

But a woman who ran a wildlife sanctuary near the coast said, when I telephoned for advice,

'Don't let her out. She won't last a moment. The other birds will kill her. Find someone with a large aviary.'

I tried and failed to find an aviary. Then I compromised. I let Pica out only when I was there to protect her. Then she went back to her cage.

One day a neighbour paid a visit. Pica, at large in the sitting-room, decided to enliven the afternoon by sitting on the visitor's head. She returned to this perch repeatedly, however often I chased her off. The man was frightened and upset. At last I opened a door and let Pica go out into the garden. Minutes later I heard the crows cawing fiercely. I hurried out. Pica had gone. I never saw her again. I searched and searched for her. I tramped the hills and the fields and woods calling her name. There was no sign of her.

I was desolate—not only at the loss of Pica but with the knowledge that I'd betrayed that affectionate and trusting bird.

Some time after she'd disappeared a neighbour said to me, 'You shoot the magpies, do you—or have them shot? They *are* a nuisance, of course,' she added kindly.

'Certainly not!' I was indignant. 'Why?'

'One came over a little while ago—I thought from your place—it looked injured—it died . . .'

'Oh!' I was shocked and very upset. 'That must have been Pica—a pet magpie—where did you find it?'

'Over there—by those bushes—but . . . it was dead . . .'

Pica used to sing in the dawn and again at sunset. She sang also as we left London each Friday night, sitting on the cushioned support behind my head. Her song was a glorious bubbling sound. She seemed blissful. In her cage, she balanced on perches and lifted her one-eyed head to pour out her praise for the world, for being alive.

No longer.

Lily and Rosie padded around the empty cage.

Rosie let me know that in her view the bird was never meant to live. It had had a good time while it lasted. But Nature won in the end, as Nature always does—and she stared directly into my face with her beautiful, honest, intelligent eyes.

45

While the high point of Caramel's day was the walk, for Maman, the greatest pleasure was what she regarded as her 'treatment', her 'physiotherapy'.

Maman's treatment consisted of a good brushing and combing very gently performed because of the painful arthritic condition of her spine. Like Caramel, because of malnutrition early in her life, Maman's bones were not well-formed, her little legs twisted, her spine severely knobbly.

She, too, was ill after she'd been at Mas des Chats a year or so. The trouble began with her decaying teeth. She couldn't and wouldn't eat. I thought she was just a tired old cat, ready to die. For a while I did nothing to help her. But then I realised she was suffering. We went to the vet. She was immediately diagnosed as having severe pain in her mouth, an inflammation of the gums from her rotting teeth, an infection which had spread to her sinuses.

She was put under anaesthesia and the bad teeth drawn, the others cleaned of tartar. Her mouth improved rapidly, but she still seemed in trouble. She had difficulty moving about and wasn't keen to eat. When her mouth was so sore, I'd been feeding her mainly on little pieces of raw liver, this being soft and easy to swallow. The chief vet, Monsieur Lamartin, came to see her. In the course of conversation I mentioned her diet of liver.

'No! No!' he raised his hand in dismay. Liver alone, he told me, does great harm to cats. Too much Vitamin A. It causes thinning of the bones, osteoporosis, which had aggravated Maman's arthritic condition. She should have meat, milk, cheese, vegetables. Liver only once a week he said. '*Crème glacée*,' he advised, 'cats like it!'

My cats didn't seem to like it—but Maman was persuaded to eat other foods. It took her a long time to get well. I nursed her, fed her like a baby, carried her out into the field twice a day to empty bladder and bowels as she found it hard to use a litter box. I gently brushed and caressed her to soothe the pain in her back. It was then that she became addicted to brushing. Long after she recovered, in fact for the

Maman was old and arthritic. She needed special care for her poor malformed bones.

rest of her life, she regarded it as her right to have a daily brushing. Purring deeply, she would change her position from side to side as I lightly brushed her, so that no square inch of her would be missed out. In addition, she had the strange little habit of licking her front paws vigorously during the brushing. She became quite well again, quite chirpy and brisk, joining the group for our late afternoon walk. She walked more sedately than the rest. I was touched to see that Baby loyally accompanied her mother, remaining with her when she would have liked to rush ahead, and escorting her home again.

46

Towards the end of my fifth year in Provence, sadness came to Mas des Chats. There were illnesses and deaths among the cats.

During those five years I'd hardly ever left the Mas for more than a day or two at a time. I would go by car to places only a few hours away—the Cevennes, Montpellier, Annecy, Geneva, Ventimiglia, the Alps, the sea.

I drove fast along the motorway to get there and hurried even faster to return. I was happy to find myself once more on the little white road that led to the Mas, happy to see the cats. And they let me know how pleased they were to see me. Bruno was particularly welcoming. He'd climb into the car as I opened the door and sit firmly and solidly on my lap.

He made it clear that he disliked my leaving them. He'd prefer it if I never went away.

There came a time, in the autumn of the fifth year, when I had to return to England for professional reasons. I went reluctantly, suffering anxiety to the point of panic beforehand. Why? I could think of no good reason.

William very kindly came to look after the cats while I was away. Other arrangements had fallen through at the last moment.

I set out uneasily with a sinking of the heart.

London was grey and cold. I walked familiar pavements, looked at familiar places, saw old friends, all with a strange indifference, a numbed spirit.

The work done, I was glad to find myself once more at London Airport. The flight left in the evening. From my seat by a window in the aircraft I looked down at the villages and towns over which we flew, little islands of lights, little human settlements in the great lonely darkness of France. The dazzle of Marseille appeared at last, then Marignane Airport with a name that has the flavour of Spain, of marigolds, Africa and oranges. William met me. He'd worked hard in my absence, doing his best to follow my instructions for the feeding of the cats.

I found them all in good order, except for Bruno. He looked ill, his coat ruffled and dull. But he was eating—almost too greedily, almost frantically.

In the late afternoon, in pale sunshine, I walked up the road, past the yellowing vines, then heard him cry. He was sitting in the road some distance behind me. I came back to him and he called to me in the voice I knew so well.

'Please pick me up.'

I remembered his first serious illness three years before when, muscles weak and tired, he used to ask me again and again to carry him. Then he was light and small. Now his great weight and size made him less easy to hold. There was, in addition, a curious limpness to his body, a lack of spring in his muscles.

In the evening I saw he couldn't jump up on the kitchen counter where he normally leaped with ease.

Next day I took him to the vet. By then he was less hungry, refusing foods which he usually enjoyed. The young vet examined him carefully. He was puzzled, I thought, as to what was wrong. I tried to explain.

'I was away. When I came back, he wasn't his normal self. He was dull and apathetic.'

'He wasn't pleased to see you?'

'Yes—he was, but he seemed tired.'

The vet gave me injections for him and pills. If he was no better in a day or two I must bring him back and leave him in the clinic for some hours for a more thorough examination.

The next day he was no better—worse, in fact. I telephoned the clinic and was told to bring him in. They would keep him until they had diagnosed his illness.

At five o'clock, Monsieur Lamartin telephoned.

'Bad news,' he said.

I waited, shocked, and afraid.

Monsieur Lamartin, used to delivering bad news, spoke briskly but kindly. Bruno had a fatal illness, feline leukaemia, similar to AIDS in humans. The diagnosis was sure and certain. His blood test proved it unmistakably. There was the faintest hope he might survive the attack

Almost to the end of his life Bruno retained his beauty, his pale fur shining, his pure blue eyes innocent and clear.

although eventually the virus would kill him. I could take him home and we would try to save him, for the moment, with antibiotics and steroids. I drove to fetch him.

An eager young girl, blonde and pretty, was at the reception desk. She knew nothing of me or of Bruno's illness.

'I've come for my cat,' I said.

Pattering ahead, she led me to the cage where Bruno lay, limp, apathetic, not stirring.

'*Ah! Qu'il est beau!*' she cried.

His beauty was radiant as ever, pale fur shining, pure blue eyes innocent and clear.

Hard pain lodged in my chest. Beautiful as he is, he will die. I put Bruno gently in his basket and drove him home. In the morning he looked shrunken, small. Pallor circled his eyes and whitened his gums.

A bright sun shone, but the air was cold. He sat for a while in the sun against the trunk of a cypress. Then I carried him into the house, upstairs to my room. That was his last walk in the garden, the last time he sat in the warmth of the sun.

Monsieur Lamartin came to vaccinate the other cats against the illness. I brought Bruno to him to ask if this was now the moment to help him die.

Monsieur Lamartin looked at him, said no, he thought there was still a chance he might overcome the virus—the faintest of chances—but it was worth the try.

His eyes, he said, were still very blue.

I only saw later that, as the illness gradually overwhelmed him, Bruno's eyes turned slowly to green, to grey.

There passed a few days of suffering. Bruno fought to live. He couldn't eat, but he drank water. I sat with him and talked to him and smoothed his ruffled coat.

I fetched him icy water from the pond where he'd always liked to drink.

Hour after hour I stayed with him. For a while, he seemed better —then worse again. Slowly he sank. He drank less, he struggled less. Then he drank no more.

Once as I stroked his face I thought he knew me. There was a flicker of life which seemed to acknowledge that all love, trust, understanding that is possible between human and cat—and cat and human—had been ours.

'I know. I remember,' he seemed to say. 'But I must go now.'

Between hope and despair, between panic and unnatural calm, I catapulted.

In the end I must call the vet again.

The young vet came, thin, tall with cropped hair and a sensitive spectacled face.

He lay on the floor where Bruno now lay and wouldn't allow me to lift him. Bruno had somehow struggled to a place where a shaft of icy air came in from the garden and the fields. It was time for him to die. There was no more hope he could live.

Gently Monsieur Chardin injected first a tranquilliser then, after a few moments, the fatal dose, and Bruno died.

'*Il est mort?*'

'*Il est mort*. Shall I take him away?'

'No—thank you—the gardener—' I couldn't speak.

'Would you like me to carry him down?'

I shook my head. I paid the fee and he went without looking back.

I was left alone with my little cat, my dear Bruno. Gently I lifted him. His tumbled body hung soft and dangling like a rag doll. I carried him down to the garden, then up over the little bridge. I dug a deep hole in a great mound of earth which Monsieur Mercier had left to use in the garden.

It was evening. Stars came out and a sickle moon. The edge of the sky was stained with the orange and green of a winter sunset.

I couldn't bear to throw the earth on Bruno's shining white body but bury him I must.

Imprisoned at last, captive in the dark, I'd never again search for him and call and call, sick with anxiety. Then when he appeared a warm flood of relief and,

'Bruno—where *have* you been?'

I'd loved him greatly. I thought my absence must have distressed him so that his resistance was lowered—and the virus which may have been in his body a long time gained the upper hand.

The other cats drifted up over the bridge, inquisitive, curious. I shouted at them to go away.

Night fell.

Monsieur Mercier dug Bruno's proper grave in the hillside above the little bridge. He covered it with flat stones and planted a flowering shrub beside it.

Baby kept asking me in her squeaky voice where Bruno was. 'Where's Bruno?' What had I done with her Bruno? Where was he, where was he?

'We'll never see him again, Baby. He's gone.'

She was sure he was there somewhere. She was desperate. She searched and searched.

She followed me everywhere, certain that where I was, Bruno would suddenly appear. Over and over again she came upstairs into the bedroom, looking for him, finding the place on the floor where he died, smelling that place over and over again.

He must be here somewhere, he must be. She stared at me with her large green eyes, eyes that insisted that Bruno would come back. She knew he would, he always had come back before.

When at last she realised Bruno would not come back, she collapsed in a small heap on a sofa and lay there, still and unmoving for hours, day after day. I became afraid. I thought she was ill, with the same illness that Bruno had had.

I picked her up. Her body had the same unresisting limpness as Bruno's and she seemed to be suffering from the same apathy and tiredness as he had done. She gave a pathetic little cry of protest as I held her and I quickly put her down again. I telephoned the vet. 'Bring her for a blood test,' suggested kind Madame Grasse.

But by the next day she was a little better. And soon she was eating again, a little at a time.

She was mourning, not ill, grieving for Bruno, as I was.

Not many months later, I had to ask Monsieur Mercier to dig another grave. Poor Rosie, too, had died. Hers wasn't the same illness as Bruno's. The diagnosis was never clear. The vet thought she'd somehow been poisoned as her symptoms were as if she'd swallowed Warfarin of a diabolically lethal variety. But I think she was ill before the acute symptoms from which she suffered shortly before her death. For a long time she'd been getting thinner and I'd noticed a little watery blood oozing from her gums. But I put that down to the fact that her teeth tended to cake with tartar. She still ate her fifteen meals a day and was as bossy and fastidious as ever. In fact, she complained of nothing. A few weeks before her death there was a cruel pallor

For a long time Rosie had been getting thinner, but she still ate her fifteen meals a day and was as bossy and fastidious as ever.

around her eyes. She became a little weak. Then she developed a profound anaemia. One day I saw she passed blood when she emptied her bowels, then there was a smudge of blood in her nostrils. Her gums also bled. It was then the vet thought she must have eaten Warfarin, perhaps in a mouse who'd been poisoned. Her body seemed unable to make new red blood cells and the blood couldn't clot. Monsieur Lamartin prescribed Vitamin K to stop the haemorrhages but she became more and more anaemic. She grew feeble. But valiant Rosie tried to carry on as before. Only she was gentler, sweeter and less critical. Then her appetite began to fail and I knew that in spite of all the care, the injections and pills, the battle was lost.

Once again I was to watch a most loved animal die. She and I went out slowly a day or two later into the garden, courageous Rosie staggering a little, her legs hardly able to carry her. She tried to run a few steps, collapsed, turned blue and gasped for breath. Her blood had become like water and there was no oxygen to sustain her.

And then she would neither eat nor drink.

Once again I telephoned the veterinary clinic. Once more the tall young man, spectacled, with close cropped hair, sensitive and gentle, knocked at the door.

There was nothing more to be done to help Rosie, except perhaps a blood transfusion. But there was not much hope that this would do more than prolong life for a few days and it would be distressing for Rosie. I chose to spare her the misery.

So it was decided to end her now suffering life.

Brave Rosie. She made one little bid to escape from the room, but I caught her and held her in my arms. She snuggled her head under my elbow as she always did when she was feeling most affectionate. She purred—and purred on until she was silenced by the tranquillising injection. And not long afterwards life was extinguished.

'*Elle est morte?*'

'*Elle est morte.*'

And he went again without a backward glance, again my tears, again a burial on the hillside and later another grave.

They lay side by side, she and Bruno—small squares of flat stone covering them, a few shrubs planted around them.

French cat and eternally English cat, I wept for them.

In my sadness I turned to Lily.

'We're the last two left,' I said, 'who remember England.'

But Lily was challenging and belligerent. Where was Rosie?

'Rosie's gone.'

Lily wasn't satisfied. Gone where?

'Where we all go, in the end. Meanwhile, you and I must stick together. We've memories in common.'

Still she challenged me, withdrew from me, suspected the worst.

'Lily,' I said, 'do you remember Hampshire? This is the time when the cuckoos are calling in the woods and the blackbirds singing, late. Do you remember the cuckoos and those evenings in the half light when the blackbirds sang until the stars came out? You and I are the only ones to remember.'

Lily's frightened and angry face accused me. Why had I taken them away? Rosie might still be alive if they'd stayed.

'Don't you like it here?'

She liked it there. Of course she remembered the cuckoos and the blackbirds—and fresh grass and English rain and Nancy's Mum and coley, of course she did.

And until Rosie had died, she'd had a companion who'd shared those memories. She would miss Rosie, she would miss her very much.

'You were never the best of friends, Lily.'

But they'd been two of a kind. They'd understood one another. She had no one now.

That was an even greater sadness for me, seeing Lily in her loneliness.

The other cats were indifferent—or sometimes even hostile to her —except for Baby, who loved everybody and who squeaked at her at mealtimes in the kitchen and gave her a brief nose-to-nose greeting.

I stretched out my hand to her.

'You have me, Lil. We must stick together. You and I remember England . . . Only you and I remember England now.'

47

The spring began, the sixth spring. Slowly the blossom unfolded, almond first and later cherry and plum, peach, apple and pear, all the great orchards alight with flowers. And the air was full of bird song. In the spring, birds flew over Provence, migrating north, stopping for a while to rest and feed—then, onwards.

For a few years, there were hardly any resident birds. People blamed insecticides, the climate, pollution, illnesses.

Then, slowly, the birds came back. In the spring following the deaths of Bruno and Rosie, there were many birds. In April and May the swallows and swifts and martins flew overhead. Some stayed and built their nests. But most of them went on to their breeding grounds in the north. In the night, with clouds passing across the sky and intermittent moonlight, I heard the sound of birds twittering and chattering overhead—a crowd of swifts, making its way from Africa to Scotland, perhaps, or Brittany or the Lake of Geneva.

The next day, early in the morning, the garden at Mas des Chats was alive with the songs of nightingales. There seemed to be a bird in every tree, in every bush. One sang especially loudly, especially full of joy, I thought. It had settled in a maple tree which stood on the edge of the terrace next to the little bridge that led to the *colline*. There it stayed and, night and morning, twittered and chuckled and burst, every now and then, into a passion of song.

At this time, the moment of life renewing, Maman died.

Poor Maman, increasingly frail and now, I think, very old, became ill with infections of various kinds. She overcame most of these with treatment by antibiotics and other medicines but she finally developed a severe chronic sinusitis which gave her difficulty in breathing and wouldn't respond to treatment. Baby detached herself from her mother at a certain point when Maman was too tired and too weak to communicate with her child. Up to this time Baby had lain beside her mother and licked her gently from head to tail. Maman enjoyed and was comforted by Baby's love, until she was too worn out to care. She no longer wanted to eat and it became clear that she must be helped to die. Monsieur Lamartin came and gave her, gently, the lethal injection.

Although Maman had hardly been noticed by the other cats towards the end of her life, her death seemed to cause agitation and disarray amongst them.

And I too mourned her and missed her greatly.

Dearest Maman. In her quiet way she had always shown me how grateful she was for all that was done for her. She seemed to know this was for the best . . .

Then there was a third little grave on the hillside.

So three cats had gone in a few months. After Maman's burial I went up the bridge and looked at the graves. Bright sunlight, spring sunlight, fell on the carefully placed flat stones.

Overhead, magpies chattered and argued. Between the branches and the leaves of the ilex trees, I saw flashes of black and white feathers and iridescent tails.

Remembering Pica and feeling tired and dispirited, I decided I'd tried too often and too hard to fight against Nature.

Perhaps, I thought, I should have allowed the abandoned and the weak to go to the wall.

I heard a faint squeak, one of Lily's uncatlike announcements.

There she was at my feet, having just got over an attack of the vapours brought on by Caramel rushing out and barking hysterically.

She needed a little meal to strengthen her. She gave me a sharp look as if to ask me what would have become of her. Didn't I think she was worth saving?

Of course you were—are, dear Lil, of course . . .

Well then . . .

She marched steadily towards the kitchen and we went into the house together. She ate carefully and finished the plateful.

A brief acknowledgement, a grateful purr, then she moved slowly back towards the open door. When she reached the doorway she sat down and began cleaning her whiskers—then stretched, relaxed,

There she was, the white Hampshire cat, in the Provençal sunshine.

turned gentler eyes towards me, purred again. She was letting me know, kindly, that she thought that after all, it was quite nice here, at Mas des Chats.

And there she was, the white Hampshire cat, in the Provençal sunlight, sitting in an open doorway (was that the ghost of Rosie who sat beside her?).

In the maple tree, the nightingale started up again, a twitter, a little run of notes, a glorious bubbling.

48

After the three deaths, the other cats seemed to lose their sense of unity. Each went his or her own way, silent and indifferent. It wasn't surprising. Bruno, as leader, had created the tensions which held them together. They'd grouped around him as he sang and danced and shouted and growled, performed his magic tricks, flirted with the girls, loved his Rosie, was man to man with Nero, stood no nonsense from Monsieur le Gris, put Oedipus in his place and kept the enemy at bay.

The remaining seven cats were confused, then drifted apart. Strange cats which hadn't previously been allowed by Bruno to come near the Mas now arrogantly wandered about on the terrace and even entered the house at night to sleep in a comfortable corner.

Bruno would have rushed forward the moment he sighted them, howled his terrifying howl, approached them at an angle like a bucking horse, spine curved, hair erect, and driven them away.

Without him the strange cats stayed. Monsieur le Gris grumbled and growled but was ineffective. Nero stared but took no action. Oedipus was frankly frightened and ran to hide.

And the females on the whole made no fuss although I sometimes heard Baby hiss and Hélène give a raucous cry.

Much later, the beautiful cats came together again.

After the deaths, the entrances. Two new cats made their appearances at about the same time, and one way and another they stayed and were adopted into the household. It was these two cats who restored unity to the group. New tensions were created, new alliances formed. One was a charming, very pretty female, Grisette, who was crazy about anything in trousers. The other was a handsome little tabby, whom we called Ben.

Ben created havoc when he first arrived by chasing all the resident cats, charging them like an Exocet missile.

The beautiful cats united in their affection for Grisette and their horrified alarm at Ben. Ben settled down eventually, accepting and accepted by the other cats. And Emilie, Hélène's daughter, returned to the house.

But before these three arrived at Mas des Chats I'd decided I needed to travel, to make a journey somewhere—anywhere!

———————◇———————

Friends came from England to look after the animals and house.

Where should I go?

The Mediterranean coast was out of the question, too noisy and crowded in high summer.

The mountains, perhaps? The eastern Pyrenees where I'd been once before? On our way there, William and I had spent a night in Perpignan. We had stayed in the best hotel but found the bedroom strange and sombre, full of dark Catalan furniture and dust. In the twilight, thousands of starlings flew into the centre of the town from the surrounding countryside. The air was thick with their wings and their cries and whistles as they quarrelled for space on the branches of the great plane trees in the streets and squares. We went from Perpignan into the mountains. There were steep and splendid views at every turn of the road and, high above, the snowfields of Mount Canigou dominated the sky. But the landscape seemed too formidable and lonely for me at that moment. I decided I wanted to see the lush green fields of the north, deep beech woods and rivers and streams and cows in grassy meadows, soft skies and the blur of rain. All this was to be found in the foothills of the Jura, a short day's journey to the north and east of Mas des Chats.

I set off driving steadily and fast. The names of the towns rolled off the motorway—Avignon, Orange, Montelimar, Valence . . .

And so to Lyons, then east and north again.

I found what I was looking for—an isolated but comfortable country hotel on the shore of a jade-green lake. All around were wooded hills, cool and shady and refreshing.

There were many walks over soft, damp fallen leaves on paths that led into the woods. Not far away, I saw, as I'd wanted to see, herds of cows in undulating, grassy meadows and also sheep, fluffy and white. These were very different from the sad, scraggy brownish sheep and goats of Provence, scratching a winter living from the mean land.

The pale blue sky was often misted with soft cloud, and once or twice it rained.

The other guests seemed to be French, mostly middle-aged Parisians, escaping for a while from the hot, polluted city. There were, I thought, many professional people among them who had come there for fresh air and quiet. The men wore panama hats and linen jackets, the women straw hats and cotton dresses. They gathered specimens of wild flowers on their walks and they had long, intense discussions with one another. They stayed for a few weeks before returning, reluctantly, to the fumes of the city.

After a week I'd had enough of the damp beech woods and the chilly green lake. The Parisians felt otherwise. I heard one woman guest complaining mournfully as a gloomy porter carried her bags to her car.

'*Tout arrive, Madame,*' he said, '*tout s'arrange et tout s'oublie.*'

I thought of this little saying as I drove down the motorway south to Provence.

Memories of the north, soft outlines blurred by mists and vapoury cloud, would probably become shadowy with time.

But images of my years in Provence would lie in my mind sharp as diamonds all my life.

The old, gentle house with rosy floors, green garden, blue and lavender hills, dark rows of cypresses, rustling canes; the waterways, the frogs and cicadas and nightingales, the radiant light, the river Rhône —and, above all, those poignant, charming animals, cats and dogs, modest in their needs, graceful, grateful, timid and brave.

I hurried to return to them. When I arrived at Mas des Chats Nero clambered into the car as I opened the door and sat heavily on my lap, and Caramel appeared, shrieking with joy. My English friends were there to greet me.

'All well,' they said, 'they missed you, of course.'

'I missed them,' I said.

49

—◇—

Late that night I decided to swim. The air was warm and calm. I drifted up and down in the mild transparent water and felt alive again.

And out of the shadows, one by one, came my cats, my seven beautiful cats, to watch me as I swam. And as always they considered me in quiet disapproval. Nero, staring with his golden eyes, willed me to get out of the pool and take him to the kitchen.

Monsieur le Gris came to the edge and gave me a pat of his strong paw as I went by. Would I never learn?

Baby let me know she thought I was crazy, but if that's what I wanted to do, so be it.

Only Katy approved. She could see it might be fun. One of these days she thought she might try it herself. I lay on my back and looked at the stars. And as I watched, a great moon, orange coloured, rose slowly up from the eastern horizon and climbed into the sky, becoming silver, becoming radiant.